I thought I had arrived. *GQ* called me a Super Christian. I had read all the right books, joined a church group, gone through the entire Bible five times, gave generously to my church, and helped the needy whenever I could. I was doing all the right things. I was light years beyond the overpaid, arrogant, stressed-out media hotshot I used to be.

I really thought I was sold out for God.
        …And then I heard about the fishermen.

I didn't know it at the time, but I was being drawn into the center of a larger-than-life adventure that would shake me out of my self-righteous complacency, rock my marriage, and bring me to my knees. But would I have the guts to risk it all and trust God to carry me through?

The Fourth Fisherman

How Three Mexican Fishermen Who Came Back From the Dead
Changed My Life and Saved My Marriage

Joe Kissack

With Allison McClymont and Al Cole

ezekiel

Published by Ezekiel 22 Productions
Atlanta, GA
www.thefourthfisherman.com

The Fourth Fisherman
www.thefourthfisherman.com

Published by Ezekiel 22 Productions
Atlanta, Georgia
information@thefourthfisherman.com
ISBN: 0-98269-120-3
Printed in the United States of America
Cover design by Ezekiel 22 Productions
Photo by Eli Beda

Table of Contents

To my wife, Carmen.
She endures.

Introduction

Years ago when I read *Wuthering Heights*, I understood what experts meant by the story-within-a-story technique. The story that begins the book and ends it, functions as just that—as a start and a finish. Usually the inner tale is stronger and more powerful than the beginning and end portions.

In 1995, Clint Eastwood directed a film called *The Bridges of Madison County* and added the same technique, which is not part of the novel from which the screenplay was taken. The "bookends" feature a brother and sister trying to make sense out of their late mother's life. Most of the film, however, revolves around Eastwood and Meryl Streep's love affair.

In 2010, I read *Sarah's Key* by Tatiana deRosnay in which one tale takes place in Paris in 1942 and the other happens more than 60 years later. As in all good story-within-a-story plots, the two separate tales converge for a satisfying ending.

I mention these three examples because it's anything but a new technique. The difference is that, as far as I know, the others planned their books or films that way. Joe didn't.

Joe Kissack's story-within-a-story came about as a surprise to the author and only after at least two years of working on the project.

After he learned about the ordeal of three Mexican fishermen, he wanted to sell it as a screenplay and also as a book called *Tres Pescadores (Three Fishermen)*. He became obsessed with the ordeal of three men who were lost at sea for longer than anyone else and survived.

Their remarkable adventure captivated Joe, and he put his energy and money into getting the book and film rights. He overcame an amazing number of personal obstacles, but he kept on.

Then something happened to Joe—hence, the story within the story. For a long time, *Tres Pescadores* consumed him, and he seemed unable to think of much else. He looked for and found God in the story. The big surprise is that Joe finally understood more than an account of three men. He saw himself in the story, and his book became *The Fourth Fisherman*.

Before he grasped the fourth-fisherman idea, Joe exhausted his savings and almost lost his marriage. That's when he realized that he was caught up in something more than *Tres Pescadores*. He couldn't separate himself from them.

This book is about the fishermen's agony and survival, or at least that's where Joe begins. But the real book, the inner story, shows readers how God took a once high-powered salesman, who was obsessed with success and image, and turned him into a new man, a dedicated husband, a serious, committed Christian.

Cecil Murphey

Cecil Murphey is the author or co-author of more than 100 books, including the New York Times' *best-seller* 90 Minutes in Heaven *(with Don Piper) and* Gifted Hands: The Ben Carson Story. *His books have given hope and encouragement to millions of people around the world.*

Prologue

When I first started to jot down some thoughts about what was happening to me as I sat alone in my room at an obscure Mexican hotel at 4 a.m., I had no idea that my cryptic and barely legible notes would one day morph into something people might actually want to read, let alone pay for. I couldn't imagine that my story was even remotely interesting up against the miraculous survival and rescue of the *Tres Pescadores*, three Mexican fishermen who were lost in the Pacific Ocean for 286 days, longer than anyone had ever been lost at sea and lived to tell about it. Their story is full of dramatic turns and impossible grace. Me, I'm just a regular guy. Sure, I've had a few top-of-the-world moments and, lately, my fair share of adventure. But next to a lost-at-sea drama of epic proportions, the story of how all this changed my life might seem a bit mundane. Except....

Except that almost every time I tell it, I get the same reaction—people lean in, sitting on the edge of their seats, their faces mirroring my emotions. I see the sadness in their eyes when I describe childhood memories I thought I had done so well to hide from the rest of the world. I see astonishment and disbelief when I lay out the story of three poor fishermen whose experience bears witness to a miracle. And then there are some people who think I've completely lost my mind. I mean, who just hops on a plane bound for Mexico in search of three strangers whose language he doesn't speak, not knowing how he's going to find them, or when he's coming home? That's what I did. You might do the same if you felt you had no other choice.

I have tried, without success, to pass this story off to people who write for a living, people who could shape it and make it worth your time, but the thing kept falling back in my lap, gnawing at me until finally I caved and started writing in earnest. I wanted to do two books. Hire professionals to write them. One would be the story of the fishermen. Big book. Big publisher. Lost at Sea. Survival. Life and Death. "Castaway" meets "The Perfect Storm" meets "The Old Man and the Sea." That book would be called *"Tres Pescadores"*—"Three Fishermen." I even bought a bunch of domain names.

The second book would be called *The Fourth Fisherman*, a nickname I was given by a journalist. This was going to be my personal faith journey, a story of a guy who could never in a million years change into a faithful Christian man. Little book. Tiny faith publisher. That was MY plan. I've had many plans. But, it wasn't THE plan. I tried like crazy to keep these two stories separate, but something kept pushing me to weave them together. And so I did.

I've heard that writing a book is like having a baby. I wouldn't know about that, though I did have some cravings. I can tell you it was wonderful, horrible, exhilarating, frustrating, and it took forever. I had to visit wormholes in my head I thought I had cemented over long ago and connect a lot of spiritual dots to illustrate the depth and wonder of the grace I've been shown. Mostly, though, I had to pray a lot and trust what I knew in my bones was right: This story needed to be told. It was no accident that I found the story of the fishermen or, rather, that their story found me. The truth is, I was once as lost as they were.

As this goes to print, there is a movie in the works based on a screenplay I wrote about these men—Jesús, Salvador, and Lucio—who say they existed on "raw fish, rainwater, and faith." I believe them. Improbably, their names translate as "Jesus," "Savior," and "Light." I will do my best to share from my heart and with a sense of humor, as accurately as I can, the unlikely series of events that brought us together and the transforming effect it had on my faith in God and my marriage.

I

The Red Carpet

I was standing on the red carpet at the Emmy Awards, wearing obscenely expensive sunglasses. Three hundred bucks worth. I had perfected the illusion. It was September of 1997, and my employment contract with Columbia Tri-Star Television was about to expire. I had been invited to fly out to LA for the awards ceremony and some meetings that would determine my next move.

I was acting like a big shot. I certainly looked the part: thousand-dollar tuxedo, cufflinks from Neiman Marcus, Rolex Oyster Day-Date, Ferragamo shoes, and, of course, the sunglasses. I was ready to rock the red carpet. I had "arrived," according to Hollywood's standards, which usually take into account one's ability to spend outrageous amounts of money on items of little substance. I'm not going to lie to you. I was one of the worst offenders, and I loved it. I was on a pretty good roll—in my tenth year with a major television studio that had promoted me five times, all the way to executive vice-president, a big salary with incredible bonuses, first-class travel (concierge level, of course), a car allowance that paid for my BMW 540i and later my Porsche 911 Carrera Cabriolet, a 6,000-square-foot house complete with a home theater and sound system that could make the hair on your legs stand up, a beautiful wife, two adorable daughters in private school, and a Harley-Davidson, just because I could.

Not bad for a small-town kid from a blue collar family in Illinois whose teenage daughters still make fun of him for having worn the same plaid shirt for his first- and second-grade class photos. (What they don't know is that I kept that shirt until fifth grade and that it was my brother's long before I ever got my hands on it.)

My road to the red carpet had not been easy. Trying to survive in the television industry was literally killing me. With an average of four shows to pitch each year, I was giving roughly 1,500 presentations annually. It wasn't rocket science, but it was incredibly nerve-wracking. I had to be "on" all the time—tens of millions of dollars were riding on it. Sure, some days it was glamorous, but the second I closed a deal, I would start stressing about the next one. Despite some of my successes—*Married with Children, Mad About You, Walker Texas Ranger, Ricki Lake*, and the big one, *Seinfeld*—every day on the job at the studio was, in my mind, another day I might be found out. I never felt I was good enough. Or that I deserved to be there. But somehow I had made a name for myself.

My job was to license the rights of television programs to broadcast stations across the country, otherwise known as syndication. Whoever figured out that television audiences would watch the same program a second, third, or even seventeenth time was a genius. Syndication is highly profitable—and cutthroat. With only so many clients in each city and 20 other shows competing for the same time slots, it was impossible to sell your show in every market. The expectation, however, was that you would. Every major studio had 15 to 20 of us. Hired guns. (I was once called a "rogue media hotshot," whatever that means. I was really just a glorified salesman.) We traveled to all 211 TV markets, four days a week, 50 weeks a year, from New York City all the way to Glendive, Montana, destined, on some level, to fail. But—and this is a big but—the money was fabulous. Even so, most of us lived beyond our means, believing that as long as the money was coming in, the physical and emotional toll was worth it. Believe me, it is very difficult to walk away.

My red carpet moment was just another part of the dance. The invitation—the whole weekend for that matter—was one more perk the studio probably knew I wouldn't, or couldn't, refuse. It was all calculated. If it were my studio, I'd probably do the same thing. They had me right where they wanted me: a guy once obsessed with a worn-out plaid shirt, from a town whose chief industries were canning peas and spinning yarn, now raking in lots of dough, rubbing elbows with American royalty, and looking like a million bucks—but unable to enjoy any of it.

One of the keys to successful red carpet walking is to do it slowly—especially the final twenty yards before you get inside. The idea is to project appreciation tinged with indifference—never gratitude, and certainly not awe. Like an old coach once told me, "Joe, if you're lucky enough to wind up in the end zone, act like you've been there before."

I tried my best to be cool, but on this day it wasn't working. For one thing, I was visibly sweating—not because it was hot but because I was about to launch into an all-out panic attack. I was on the crest of a career high, having a good hair day, wearing the aforementioned sunglasses, wishing I could teleport from the privacy of our car, over the red carpet, to the anonymity of my seat inside the Pasadena Civic Auditorium. Instead, I skated arm in arm with my wife, Carmen, down the red carpet, desperate to reach the cool darkness of the theater, while my colleagues watched from behind, in all likelihood bewildered by my behavior.

Looking back, I can see that the wheels were starting to come off. I was fried and I knew it. Earlier that week I had met with the head of television for the studio, and he asked me that classic interview question, "Where do you see yourself five, ten, or fifteen years from now?" I told him I wanted his job someday. It was positively ludicrous to think I could handle this guy's responsibilities. He was really smart and operated as if ice water ran through his veins. It sounded good when I said it, though, and it was probably what he wanted to hear.

Part of me really wanted to stay; it was what I knew. But I was tired of the pressure. I was toast. The industry was intense: the farther you advanced up the ladder, the fewer the jobs—no lateral moves. It was all about the next job, and there were only about six jobs at my level in the entire studio system. There was no workplace Zen in 1997. It was all tension, all the time. If you weren't stressed and strung out, you would be replaced. Some guys could handle it, the thousands of canned speeches, smiles, fake laughter, and contracts. I couldn't anymore. I was stuck. Everything I held dear was riding on my success: my house, my car, my family's future, my reputation—my sunglasses. The moment I stepped off that tightrope, it would all be gone, handed to the next guy in line.

Years earlier, Carmen had urged me to see a psychiatrist. She said she was tired of seeing me this way, a shell of my former self, coming home in the middle of the day just to escape. She was worried that I was being ground down to nothing. She didn't understand why I kept renewing my contract. I suppose I was looking for validation, approval, something to fill me up. When I shared this with the psychiatrist, he looked into my eyes and said, "Tell me about your dad." No one had ever gone there, and I didn't know what to say. So I never went back. The short version is that I finally crashed and burned, found God—sort of—and began to see myself as reborn.

I thought I had arrived. Ten years after my red carpet experience, *GQ* called me a Super Christian. I had read all the right books, joined a men's group, gone through the entire Bible five times, gave generously to my church, and helped the needy whenever I could. I was light years removed from the overpaid, arrogant, stressed-out media hotshot I used to be. I really believed I was sold out for God.

...And then I heard about the fishermen.

I didn't know it at the time, but I was being drawn into the center of a larger-than-life adventure that would shake me out of my self-righteous complacency, rock my marriage, and bring me to my knees. But would I have the guts to risk it all and trust God to carry me through?

2

The Fishermen

Shortly before sunrise on October 28, 2005, five fishermen boarded a 27-foot open fiberglass boat that resembled an oversized skiff and left San Blas, a small village on the western coast of Mexico. They silently pushed their *panga* away from shore and headed out to get fuel, stopping briefly to fill a dozen large plastic containers with gasoline. The captain had assembled his crew just a day or two before the trip, so most of the men were unacquainted and quiet when they stocked the boat with what they would need for the trip. With luck, they would fish the boat full in three days, maybe four. Just to be safe, they packed enough sandwiches, canned tuna, and bottled water to last them four days, along with some blankets and extra clothes. A day's worth of fishing might yield each man two hundred pesos, about twenty dollars.

Juan David Lorenzo (known to the men as Señor Juan) is in his mid-forties, just over six feet tall and heavyset. He worked in Mazatlan repairing computers and installing networks. "Juan was a simple fishing enthusiast, a man who likes adventure," his brother, Daniel, would later tell a reporter from *Televisa*, a local TV network. "The ocean fascinated him." Daniel said Juan often disappeared for long periods and dismissed the rumors of drug-trafficking. "My brother was not living that kind of life," he said. "What he earned he got from computers."

Salvador Ordonez, 37, is about five feet tall, with very dark skin and a sad face. He is a gentle man but tough as nails. He has been a fisherman for nearly thirty years, learning to fish on the East coast of Mexico in the Gulf. He started fishing for sharks in his teens and ended up in San Blas about fifteen years ago. He has a deep faith in God and brings a Bible with him whenever he fishes. Salvador believes he is granted life on a daily basis by a Creator who controls the land and sea, and he says he is more at home on the sea than on land.

Lucio Rendon, 27, 6-foot-4, looks like a Mayan warrior without the intensity. He has lived with his grandmother, his *panchita*, since age 10, along with four of his uncles in her dirt floor, four-room, 600-square-foot faded lime-green cinderblock hut. The six of them sleep on cots in one room, and there is a small living area and a bathroom with a hole for a toilet. Another room houses a shrine to the Virgin Mother. They live in El Limon, a village of two hundred people, fifteen miles inland from San Blas. Everyone Lucio knows is a fisherman. He quit school at 13 and learned how to fish from his uncle Remigio. Lucio typically walks or hitches a ride to the nearest fishing village, Boca del Asadero, about five miles away, disappearing for days or weeks at a time looking for work as a day laborer on a small boat. A year earlier, he worked with Salvador for a few days before they got stranded on an island when their engine failed.

Jesús Vidana, 27, 5-foot-10, is ruggedly handsome with light-colored skin. Like Lucio, he moves from town to town in search of work on small fishing boats. He lives about eight hours north of San Blas in a one-room shack he built out of sticks and scraps of lumber. The shack has no electricity or running water, and the interior walls are covered with cardboard for insulation. A queen-size bed sits in one of the corners, and the floors are ground loose dirt and sand that give the appearance of powdered brown sugar. On extremely hot nights, Jesús uses an electric fan that rests on an old milk crate, with a 100-foot extension cord stretching to his nearest neighbor's house. He lives with his pregnant wife, Jocelyn, and his son, Juan, who is almost three. Jesús has a huge smile and an incredible singing voice to go along with his acute sense of humor. With a little coaching, he could have his own variety show on TV.

Farsero, the mysterious one, is skinny and older than the rest of the crew, though his exact age is not known. He is a very tough guy. Señor Juan introduced him to the other men only as *"El Farsero,"* which means "The Joker," though he rarely smiled or said much. When anyone would press him, he would say, "You don't need to know anything else." The few times he initiated a conversation, it was with Señor Juan and not the other three. After the rescue, there was speculation that Farsero never existed because no friends or relatives ever came forward to ask about him, and the three survivors could provide little information about him. The press tried to make a big deal out of this, but it's not unusual that men who work together in rough conditions keep to themselves and volunteer little about their personal lives. ("Hey, Rocky, hand me that blowtorch, and if you don't mind, could you tell me about your childhood wounds?" *Yeah, right. These guys are only there for the work and have no interest in making friends.*)

Señor Juan was not a professional fisherman, but he owned a boat, an engine, and a fishing net, which made him captain. He hired Farsero, Jesús, Salvador, and Lucio to do the hard work that fishing in this part of the world requires. These men do not use fishing rods. There is no depth-finder. No lifejackets. No radio. No bikini cover to protect them from the sun. Except for an outboard motor and a fiberglass hull, this is about as primitive as it gets.

Their *panga* has a V-shaped hull that is nine feet wide and five feet deep, with four three-foot-tall dividers that split the interior into five sections. There is an enclosed area in the bow for storage. In addition to food, blankets, and a few extra clothes, they had on board a cooler filled with ice, shark knives, a whetstone, rope, and an anchor. This particular *panga* had an added feature: a welded flotation chamber that provides extra buoyancy so the craft can carry a larger load of fish.

As day was breaking behind them, the five fishermen headed past the harbor master's shack and out of the channel. Señor Juan turned the *panga* west toward the Islas Marias, which lay sixty miles ahead. He gunned the engine and the front end of the boat rose out of the calm Pacific waters. The other four men nestled against the inner walls of the boat, preparing for a long ride.

3
The Paddle

"Go get me the paddle," my dad would say. We weren't going canoeing. I was about nine years old when it started, usually over some innocuous incident typical of a kid my age, like telling a fib, throwing a tantrum, or spelling my name on the driveway with butane and setting it on fire. Okay, when I was five, I did stab my brother in the leg with a pair of scissors, but I had no idea that leg skin was so soft.

In our house, discipline was doled out with my dad's fraternity paddle, which lived on top of the refrigerator with the dust bunnies and cigarettes until summoned into action, usually about ten or twelve times a year. I think the very first trip I made from the fridge after I got the paddle was when I started to learn how to mask the pain. I tried everything—rerunning episodes of *Hogan's Heroes* or *The Munsters* in my head, playing imaginary games of basketball where every shot went in, trying to convince myself that the pain was only temporary. What-

ever it took, I did it, and by the time I was grabbing my
ankles, I couldn't feel a thing. Neither of us spoke during
these sessions. The only sound was my dad paddling. His
goal was not only to impress upon me certain letters of
the Greek alphabet, but also our family's cardinal rule:
Never mess up.

I think I had it easier than my older brothers and my
sister, who endured a less-mellow version of my father and
grew great, ugly tumors of loathing for a man who even
now remains mostly oblivious to the pain and damage he
caused. I was the baby: strong, agreeable, and apparently
full of promise to a dad hell-bent on raising a quarterback. I was competitive, too, adding my name to the
roster of every sports league that my little town had to
offer, partly to please my father, but mostly for the opportunity to hit back, to rage and rush and pound in ways
legitimized by a referee and uniforms. Football was ideal
for this. I wanted to be a linebacker like Dick Butkus.
Unfortunately, I was told I had to be a quarterback.
*Quarterback? No. Not quarterback. They don't get to hit people.
Fran Tarkenton was a quarterback. I didn't want to be Fran
Tarkenton. I wanted to be Dick Butkus.*

Naturally, I was a lousy quarterback and everyone
knew it, especially my dad, who rarely missed a chance to
remind me. But I was good at making people laugh, which
was a great way to hide the mess inside. So I mostly hung
out with people who got my jokes or didn't mind being
the butt of them. When I was with them, I could feel
good enough, even if it was only for a few minutes at the
lunch table.

In this tiny town, you didn't hate your father. Even if you did, you never said so. You went out for football, kept your nose to the grindstone, and, if you were lucky, you got a good job at the yarn factory. I continued to defend him to the rest of my family and the town at large for the longest time, as sons who long for their father's approval tend to do. Today, I believe my dad did the best he could. He was a small-town baseball, football, and basketball coach who just wanted his kids to be winners. He was a carpenter in the summers. I guess everything looked like a nail to him and he was the hammer. I just never knew which side of him was going to show up on any given day.

He did try to connect with me through golf. In high school, I was winning a match in the club championship, and I was up by three holes with four left to play when he came out on the course and started to tell me how I wasn't doing something right. When I asked him to leave, he got angry and stormed off. I lost the match on the final hole. That night when he got home after a few too many, he came marching into the family room, swinging. I put my arms up around my head, like a boxer who is just trying to survive the round. My mom had been cutting his hair and was right on his tail holding a pair of scissors like a switchblade, trying to protect me. He popped me a few times, and my mom started yelling that she was calling the police. All I remember is that he stopped.

When I was 17, he started taking me with him on his motorcycle trips, an attempt, I suppose, at father-son bonding. We would ride out on the new blacktop, stop at every white-trash bar along the way, and sit together in silence while I perfected a new way to cover up my pain, popping top after top of Old Milwaukee until I was numb. Then we would ride home. Ironically, he had shattered his paddle on my calloused behind a year earlier, beating me for the very thing he was now encouraging. All of a sudden I was his drinking buddy. No wonder I have issues.

4
On The Pacific

When the *panga* neared the Islas Marias, Señor Juan cut the engine. The men began to unfurl the fishing net, the *cimbra*, as they had done hundreds of times. A *cimbra* is made by hand from fine but strong nylon fibers and floats horizontally about twenty feet below the surface of the water, suspended by beat-up buoys that have flag-sticks attached to them to signal other boats to steer clear. This particular *cimbra* extended for nearly two miles. Once the net is in place, the boat slowly zigzags across the water, snagging any sea life that happens to be in the wrong place at the wrong time.

Attached to the bottom of the *cimbra* and spaced about every thirty feet, ten-foot-long wires carry three-inch shark hooks that are sometimes baited with fish. Above each shark line, on the surface, a float—usually a plastic soft drink bottle—serves as a marker. When a fisherman sees any sort of commotion in the net, he pulls the net in toward the boat. If there is something of value, say, a shark or a tuna—they yank it out of the net, throw it in the belly of the boat, and hit it on the head with a club. Occasionally, something will get caught in the net that is of no use or might damage the *cimbra*, which is more valuable than the boat—about $3,000 U.S., more than a year's wages for most crew members. For example, if a sting ray were to get caught in the net, one of the crew would take off all of his clothes, grab a shark knife, dive into the water, and slice off the "wings" of the animal with surgical precision so as not to damage the net, even as the sting ray is trying to kill him.

Most fishermen in this part of the world have been doing this since second grade. Their brothers do this. Their sisters are married to men who do this. Their fathers do this. Uncles, grandfathers, great-grandfathers as far back as anyone can remember do this. Mostly, though, they sit and wait and watch the markers for any movement. Sometimes they make small talk; sometimes they doze off. When nature calls, they relieve themselves by hanging off the back of the boat and dragging their butts in the water. No paper required.

The first day out, the five fishermen caught nothing of any consequence. Just past midnight, a shift in the wind woke Salvador, who is also known as "Chava." Moving rapidly toward them was a wall of black clouds five miles high. Salvador woke the other men, but Señor Juan and Farsero were unconcerned about the approaching storm. Within a few minutes, the wind was howling and quickly escalated to forty miles per hour, producing fifteen-foot swells that tossed the boat and its contents around like Ping-Pong balls in a lottery drawing. Flashes of lightning lit up the night sea. Salvador knew that each monstrous wave carried the threat of death: If the *panga* were to capsize or if the men were swept overboard, there was little chance they would survive.

One swell lifted the boat thirty feet high and brought it down with a thunderous crash, stretching the *cimbra* beyond its breaking point and snapping the line like a ripe string bean.

"Why didn't you tie the line right?" Señor Juan screamed at Salvador.

"You're the captain!" he responded angrily. "You should have checked it yourself." Salvador stood in the center of the boat, up to his chest in icy seawater, his eyes burning. When the storm finally subsided, the *cimbra* was nowhere in sight. A tattered rope was all that remained.

"We will find the line," growled Señor Juan.

Jesús, Salvador, Farsero, and Lucio tried to reason with him, suggesting that they try to reach land and come back later to look for the net, but Señor Juan refused. He continued the search for two days, frantically circling and criss-crossing the area, draining most of their fuel supply. They eventually spotted another boat in the distance and headed for it, but before they got halfway there, the engine sputtered and died. Not wanting to get their fishing lines tangled, the men in the other boat started their engine and pulled away. There were no other boats in sight. Most of them had returned to port ahead of the storm. The *panga* was drifting now, caught in the westward-moving Pacific current.

Salvador could still see one of the Marias Islands, but the strong current was pushing their small fishing boat out to sea. Tempers began to flare. The fishermen soon realized, however, that the missing *cimbra* was the least of their problems. The storm had washed away some of the tools and all of the canned food. A few bottles of water and a couple of sandwiches remained, along with their shark knives, some extra clothes, a few blankets, and Salvador's Bible. Exhausted from two days of searching for the *cimbra*, the men slept soundly.

When Salvador opened his eyes the next morning, he stood up and looked around. He saw nothing but water in every direction. Then he woke the other men. They all knew they were lost.

5
On Campus

The first time I saw Carmen she was wearing blood-red penny loafers, a yellow button-down shirt, and khakis. She was stunning. I didn't hear or see anything else. I watched her glide across the room and, to my dismay, sit next to my six-foot-four, 280-pound roommate, Pee-Wee. He and I were going into our senior year and were part of a group of University of Iowa students who had volunteered to help returning alumni have a good time at their class reunion. I figured it would be a good addition to my resume, and I could use the free yellow shirt they gave us.

I was just about to jump across the table and force myself between this mystery girl and Pee-Wee when he mumbled something to her that made her laugh. I was ready to hit the panic button. He said something else to her. She laughed again. One more joke from him and I would be toast. It didn't help that he was moderately good-looking. I sat there plotting my strategy. *How am I going to wedge myself between them?* When the meeting was over, Pee-Wee was out the door with her in a flash. By the time I got to the hallway, they were nowhere to be found.

"Another One Bites the Dust" played in my head until I got home that night. I was consoling myself with my daily Little Debbie bar when Pee-Wee walked into our apartment.

"You know that girl I left the meeting with?" he said casually. "She wanted to know if I knew the guy with 'the dreamy brown eyes.'"

What? Could it be? Yes! She was talking about me!

I sat him down and interrogated him. *Where is she from? How old is she? What does she like? C'mon, man! I need this information!* A few days later, I spotted the short-haired beauty I thought I had lost to the big fella. She was with her roommate, Leigh Ann, but all I could see was Carmen. I walked over and blocked their path.

"I'm going to marry you," I blurted out, surprising even myself.

"I don't even know you," Carmen said.

"Well, why don't you go out with me and get to know me?" I asked.

"I have a boyfriend," she said, which momentarily threw me off stride.

"Oh," I said, trying to disguise the angst I was feeling. I vaguely remember saying something along the lines of "I guess I'll see you around then" and walked off.

But having been so close to her, I knew that somehow—boyfriend or not—I had to find a way to make her mine. I asked my friend Kevin, a budding investigative journalist, to track down Carmen's phone number. He came back with Leigh Ann's number instead, so I called her and asked her to put in a good word about me to Carmen.

In spite of my "I'm going to marry you" pre-emptive proposal, she called me back and agreed to have drinks with me. (For the record, I never used that line on any other girl.) The day after our first date, she told me she liked my sense of humor and later told me she was disappointed that I didn't kiss her goodnight. The truth is, I didn't want to scare her off, so I went the other direction completely—completely hands (and lips) off. I was out of my mind in love. I waited two days and called again to see if we could get together. This time we kissed. It was skyrockets in flight.

There was one problem: her boyfriend. He was handsome—and ripped. I weighed 147 pounds dripping wet. During the weeks after I first met Carmen, we saw each other sporadically. One night we were on a walk and we stopped by a park and walked over to the swings. While we were swinging, I decided to put my foot down.

"I don't want you to date anyone else," I said firmly, expecting to hear something like, "You seem like a really nice guy, but...," or "I think we should just be friends," or, worst of all, "I'm sorry. I just got engaged."

"I broke up with him today," she said with little fanfare. My ears must have been on a tape-delay, because I barged right ahead.

"There is just no way I can continue to see you if you won't see me exclusively." *Did she just say that she broke up with him today? For me? Before I even asked her to?*

After that, we went everywhere and did everything together. I suppose we were destined to be married. All I thought about was how much I wanted to be with Carmen. She was warm, muffiny goodness, and I felt loved, maybe for the first time in my life. And she laughed at my shtick. Having a beautiful girl love you and laugh at your jokes is about all a guy really needs.

Fall semester started, and it seemed like time for me to meet her parents. I'm pretty sure this wasn't my idea. We drove to her hometown from Iowa City on a Friday to see her brother play in a high school football game. I met her mom and dad, and it seemed to go just fine. At least they didn't seem too bothered by my being there.

The next day was like the part in *Dumb and Dumber* where Lloyd imagines everything going his way. Carmen and I went to the club where she had been a lifeguard. We visited her high school and saw some of her old friends. We drove by the Maytag washer and dryer factory, then went to the Maid-Rite where we ate loose-meat sandwiches, finally ending up at the appliance store her mom and dad owned. It was like a John Cougar Mellencamp song: *Ain't that America for you and me...Little pink houses....*

I had two job offers out of college: Maytag and the Carnation Milk Company. Maytag was based in Carmen's hometown, so we quickly crossed that one off the list because she didn't want to stay there, and I think we both knew we would wind up together. Carnation offered me a job in Charlotte, and I said yes.

I had hit it big, man. Nineteen-five a year and a company car (a two-year-old Chevy Citation). I had three brand-new suits from Ewers Men's store (I had worked there while I was in college), two pairs of wingtips (one black, one brown) and a Sears credit card. I was hauling in nineteen-five. I thought I was rich. Nineteen-five, baby. I thought it was enough to buy anything and everything I could ever want. (It took me a few years to pay off the Sears card. That vacuum cleaner wound up costing me about two thousand bucks.)

Carmen and I had a great summer together. But summer ended and she had to go back to school for her senior year. When she left, I was a mess. I was terrible at my job, and I wasn't too fond of my boss, who thought he was General Patton. And I was very lonely. I only had two friends—Pat and Greg. They were fun guys who worked in the TV business, and they invited me to do stuff with them, mostly stuff that involved drinking beer.

I would call Carmen every few days in tears and beg her to visit me. She would come for the weekend, and then go home, and then I would cling to Pat and Greg. One Saturday afternoon, we carried Pat's TV down to the pool and watched football all day while we drank beer. I had to study my product line. General Patton would be quizzing me on Monday about the price of a six-ounce can of Mighty Dog versus the ten-ounce can.

"Hey, you might be good at what Greg and I do," Pat said out of the blue. "We sell TV time."

"TV time?" *I love TV. TV sets. TV commercials. TV dinners. I could do anything that has anything to do with TV,* I thought.

He set up an interview for me, and I put on my best suit and the black wingtips. They had really cool offices near the mall, and his company car was a Cutlass Sierra. Man, what I wouldn't do to have a Sierra!

His boss said they might have an opening in Atlanta. One day that next week, I called in sick and drove there to meet the manager, who said I seemed like the "right cut of cloth." He must have liked my blue suit and my wingtips. Two weeks later, I moved to Atlanta.

6

Blood Brothers

The fishermen had been drifting for about four days. All of the food and water was gone. Jesús' last supper was whatever he could squeeze from his tube of toothpaste the night before.

"We have God above us, watching over us," Salvador told the others, trying to reassure them. He was confident they would survive. "He is always with us. We have a Bible. We have to pray." Salvador's Bible was special to him. When he was a young man, he had often gotten into trouble. During one of these escapades, a friend of his was badly injured. The doctor said he would never walk again. Every day while he was in the hospital, Salvador's friend read the Bible his parents had given him. He told Salvador he had confessed his wrongdoing to God, promised to do his best in the future, and trusted that God was going to perform a miracle—he believed he would walk out of the hospital on his own two legs. Salvador agreed that this would be a great blessing, but he watched his friend endure weeks of physical therapy without any progress.

When the day came to leave the hospital, Salvador's friend rolled himself toward the exit in a rickety old wheelchair. Suddenly, one of the wheels came off, stopping the chair dead in its tracks. Salvador watched in amazement as his friend lifted himself out of the chair, took a step toward the door, and walked out of the hospital just as he had said he would. The friend told Salvador that if he would believe in the power of God, miracles were available for him. He handed his Bible to Salvador as a gift.

The other men did not know the story of Salvador's Bible, and Señor Juan did not appear to share Salvador's faith. He sat against the edge of the boat for days on end doing little. Farsero often mimicked Señor Juan's pouting. Salvador was slowly becoming the captain by default, Jesús his second in command, and Lucio a sometime helper and official timekeeper because he had a $20 Casio watch with a day-date calendar. On the first night after they realized they were lost, Lucio looked at the watch. It was ten minutes to seven. After what felt like two hours had passed, he looked at it again—it was five minutes to seven.

Salvador assigned jobs to the men that could help them pass the time and give them a sense of purpose. Jesús and Lucio were to watch for passing boats. Two days later, they spotted two enormous oil tankers on the horizon and started yelling and waving their arms. All of the men took off their shirts and waved them furiously, screaming at the top of their lungs. They had no doubt that someone on one of the tankers would see them. But even if someone had been looking for a small boat, it would have been impossible to see it from that distance.

Going for days without liquid was making it difficult for the men to swallow. It felt as if they were ingesting tiny shards of glass. Seawater appeared to be their only option, but Salvador, who had taken a survival course a year earlier in San Blas, knew it would be a mistake. The other men decided to take their chances. They dipped their shirts into the water, lifted them over their open mouths, and wrung out some of the seawater.

Salvador cut off a chunk of a plastic gas container with a shark knife to make a cup. Then he lowered his pants.

"What are you doing?" asked Jesús in disbelief.

"I want to live," responded Salvador. "I am going to drink this—to survive." Salvador relieved himself into the cup, raised it to his lips, and drank.

"I'm not drinking mine!" said Lucio, laughing.

It wasn't long before Lucio and Jesús suffered the effects of drinking the seawater. Lucio described the pain as being stuck in the back and head with thousands of needles. His stomach ached so badly at times that he cried. Realizing they could not drink any more seawater, Lucio and Jesús swallowed their pride and drank their own urine.

Fortunately, the fishermen soon found themselves covered by a misty drizzle, and they created a makeshift gutter system off the bow enclosure, washing out the empty gasoline containers to collect as much rainwater as they could. They took turns sleeping during the day under the protection of the bow enclosure or under blankets. At night they could see the lights of ships miles in the distance, but it was useless to try to signal them.

They occasionally would hear an aircraft overhead, but there was no chance that anyone gazing out a window from thirty-thousand feet, even on a clear day, would see them. The men often wondered if anyone back home had noticed they were missing. It wasn't unusual for any of them to be out of touch with their families for extended periods. Lucio's Uncle Remigio, however, did go to San Blas and ask around if anyone had seen his nephew lately. He also checked with San Blas harbor officials, who said they had no record of a boat leaving with Lucio on board.

"Of course there isn't a record," Remigio told them. "They would have snuck out in the dark, because they were too poor to buy a fishing permit." The authorities said they would do what they could, but they weren't going to waste fuel looking for him on the water when it was just as likely that Lucio was spending a few days partying with friends, which he would do on occasion.

Señor Juan was still technically in charge, but Salvador was the one leading the effort to stay alive. Without food or water, the only nourishment the men got was from the Bible and from Jesús repeating over and over that they would soon be rescued. Lucio was becoming angry at everything, especially the boats that didn't see them. It had only been a few weeks, but he was starting to come unhinged.

Going for so long without food and so little water was wearing on all of the men, but when the temperature cooled down in the evenings, they would wake up and make small talk. Even though Señor Juan had tried to attach blame for the loss of the *cimbra*, the other men forgave him for using up all the fuel searching for it. They understood how valuable the net was and that, as captain and owner of the boat, he had the right to give the orders. Besides, it wasn't going to do anybody any good to harbor ill feelings. Salvador could see that Señor Juan was suffering more than the rest, so he made a special effort to comfort him. One evening Salvador moved to the back of the boat where Señor Juan was leaning against the side staring into the water.

"Chava, look," Señor Juan whispered, pointing to a spot in the sea twenty feet away. "A *caguama* (turtle)." In a flash, Salvador was out of the boat and into the water. Lucio and Jesús were startled by the splash and rushed to the back of the boat to see what was happening. Farsero didn't move. Salvador grabbed hold of the shell of a forty-pound sea turtle. He had done this sort of thing before, but never without eating anything for thirteen days and in a current that was moving faster than he could swim. He knew that if he got too far from the boat, he wouldn't be able to make it back. Salvador also knew that the turtle was about to dive hard. He tried to flip the turtle over, but before he could do it the turtle took him for a ride eight feet below the water. When he and the turtle resurfaced, Salvador kicked his legs frantically trying to get back to the boat, still clutching the shell. Jesús and Lucio cheered him on, waiting at the edge of the boat with shark knives and what was left of the tattered rope that had held the *cimbra*. Salvador pushed the turtle to the edge of the boat, and Lucio looped the rope around one of its front flippers. Jesús grabbed the other flipper, and they lifted their next meal into the boat. Then they reached down and pulled Salvador in.

Jesús sliced off a flipper and gave it to Salvador, who licked the blood as if he were licking an ice cream cone. Lucio grabbed the knife, cut off the turtle's head, and tossed it aside, even as its jaws were still snapping. He lifted the turtle's carcass and tipped it over the edge of an improvised bucket, causing a thick stream of blood to pour out.

"We will have to drink it while it is still hot," said Salvador. "It will thicken quickly if we don't." Salvador passed the bucket to Señor Juan, who put up his hand to refuse it. Then he offered it to Farsero, who also declined. Salvador took a swig and gave it to Lucio, who gulped it down like a chocolate milkshake, blood dripping from the corners of his mouth.

"*Vampiro!*" Jesús shouted, laughing at Lucio. "Let me have some." Jesús threw his head back and drank the turtle blood. He was surprised by the sweetness of it. Jesús gave the bucket to Salvador, who again offered it to Señor Juan and Farsero. This time Señor Juan sniffed it, closed his eyes, took a sip, and swallowed. He immediately jumped up and spit it over the side. Then he began to gag and vomited into the water.

Meanwhile, Jesús was ripping the turtle to pieces as the steaming hot flesh oozed blood. He rinsed the raw meat with seawater and gave it to Salvador, who carved it up like a Thanksgiving turkey. They devoured every bit of it—intestines, fat, eyeballs. They sucked the jelly-like marrow from the bones and scraped the shell clean. Jesús, Lucio, and Salvador enjoyed their meal of rare meat and could not understand why Señor Juan and Farsero would not eat it. It would be two weeks before any of them would eat again.

Birds, most likely Blue-footed or Masked Boobys, occasionally landed on the edges of the boat and on the bow enclosure. Salvador would sit quietly with his shirt in his hands and wait, like a tiger ready to pounce on its prey. Having had little exposure to humans this far out at sea, the unsuspecting birds were no match for him. In one lightning-quick motion, he would trap a bird in his jacket, snap its neck, then announce that breakfast would soon be served. Jesús was so impressed by Salvador's ability that he nicknamed him *"El gato,"* which means "the cat." After plucking the feathers, Jesús, Salvador, and Lucio would eat everything but the bones, including the duck-like webbing on the bird's feet. Farsero and Señor Juan gagged on the raw bird meat and gave up trying to eat it.

In early December, the men noticed that barnacles had formed on the bottom of the boat. The barnacles contained bits of food that attracted turtles and smaller fish. The smaller fish, of course, attracted bigger fish. From this point on, food was plentiful. But there would be little rain through the end of February. So the fishermen drank the blood of the sea turtles to stay hydrated.

"We would cut off their heads," Jesús would say in a post-rescue interview, "and drink from them like chalices."

7
Soul Mates

I had been in the TV job in Atlanta for about six weeks, and I was ready to make my next big move. I bought a marquis-shaped diamond engagement ring. Carmen was coming to visit to check out internships, but I had a longer commitment in mind. I shared my plans with some of my co-workers, who seemed nice enough and would eventually become my family in Atlanta. But they were very intense about selling TV advertising. After work one day, one of the guys who had taken me under his wing asked me to go out for drinks.

"This isn't my idea," he said as we were driving to the bar, "but everyone in the office has nominated me to tell you we don't think you should get married. You're too young, and this job is hard on marriages. The long hours. The entertaining." They didn't even know Carmen. They didn't really know me. I told him that I knew what I was doing and that they all should keep their noses out of my business. I didn't need them telling me how to live my life. I loved her, and I was going to marry her. End of conversation.

"I've delivered the message," he said, shrugging his shoulders. "Now let's get some cocktails." I assume he went back and told my colleagues that I had rejected their advice. A short time later, though, Carmen came to town, and everyone at the office went out of their way to be gracious to her.

I picked Carmen up at the airport and tried to find the park I had found on a map. I had a picnic basket in the trunk with some chilled wine and roasted chicken, the whole schmear. I was trying to act very cool until I realized I couldn't find the park, and then I started to get mad.

"It's okay," Carmen said. "We can just go back to your apartment."

"No!" I said much louder than I meant to. "This has to be just right." Very subtle.

She knew right away. Two hours later, I found the park and pulled out the warm wine, the cold chicken, and a jewelry box.

"Will you marry me?"

"Yes." 1.4 seconds. Done.

Her mom helped us with everything we had to do for the wedding. Her dad was happy when the bar opened. We got some cool gifts (including a pair of Chuck Taylor high-tops and a shoehorn) and went to Mexico for our honeymoon where I got sick as a dog. We came back to a brand-new condominium with new furniture and two new cars. I had a great job in TV and Carmen had gotten her dream job: flight attendant. She was 22 and I was 23, and we didn't have a clue. We were both from small towns, went to school in small towns. We didn't know anything about anything. Most of the other men in my family got married right out of high school, so I figured I had really taken my time.

I worked two years in that first TV job before another TV company offered me twice as much money. I jumped at the opportunity. Two years later, the studio offered to double my salary, so I jumped again. Then we moved to company headquarters in Los Angeles. I persuaded Carmen to give up her job and we headed west. We lived in a little bungalow in the valley near the studio.

One day when I was on the road selling a show called *227,* I checked into a hotel in Colorado Springs. The bellman opened the door to my room, and I saw a little teddy bear on the bed with a ribbon attached to two balloons filled with helium—one pink and one blue. *What a cute gift for the guests,* I thought. *Too bad I don't have kids.* I walked over to the bed and read the card:

We are in the pink...or...the blue
Love,
Carmen.

It took me about 15 seconds to get it. "Oh, my!" I said, turning to the bellman for a reaction. "I'm going to be a father!"

He was not moved. "Where would you like your bag?" he asked.

I called Carmen and we both squealed with joy. Then I headed down to the hotel bar, listened to some ragtime on the player piano, drank beer from a giant flute, and went to bed.

We had been in LA for about two years and saw that it was nothing like the middle-America environment we grew up in and wanted to raise our kids in. When I discovered that every major studio but ours had an office in Dallas, I put together a presentation for my boss to show him why we needed one. I was traveling to Dallas every week anyway, so it made perfect sense to live there. Carmen happened to have a doctor's appointment on the day of my presentation. I got up early, went to the office and rehearsed the presentation, then met with my boss. Carmen called later that morning to tell me she was ready to go to the doctor. I looked at my watch.

"Honey, the appointment isn't for another two hours," I said.

"We need to go now."

"In a couple of hours the traffic won't be so bad," I said.

"I need to go *now*."

"But...."

"Joe, you need to come home right now!"

"What?...Oh boy!...Are you?...Is it happening?"

"Just come get me as soon as possible," Carmen said calmly.

I rushed home and found her sitting in the kitchen in the dark with her suitcase next to the back door and our dog, Ginger, the crazy brown-spotted Dalmatian, at her side. Ginger had no idea when we left her that day that when we returned, she would no longer be our baby. She would just be a dog.

"How was your presentation?" Carmen asked.

"What?...Oh...Good, I guess...Where's your suitcase?"

"It's right here," she said, pointing at it.

"Should we go straight to the emergency room? Should I call an ambulance?" My head was spinning and Carmen's contractions were coming regularly, several minutes apart.

"I already talked to the doctor's office," she said. "They said to come there first." She told me her contractions had been fairly steady since 4 a.m.

"Why didn't you tell me this morning?" I growled.

"I didn't want to worry you before your presentation," she said. I had already forgotten about that. Important marriage note: Wife in labor trumps presentation.

We made the trip to Cedars Sinai in record time and got a private labor and delivery room that was nicer than our house—hardwood floors, TV with VCR, private bath and shower. The Hollywood sign was visible from our window. In those days insurance paid for the best, and they paid 100 percent. *We could vacation here*, I remember thinking.

Carmen's labor pains were coming more frequently, and I was coaching just like they had shown us in Lamaze class. She was determined not to have any drugs and was working hard through each contraction. Then she suddenly stalled out. The doctor told us to walk around the hospital floor to get things going again, so they hooked her up to a portable IV stand and we headed out. When we stopped to rest, I stepped into the visitors lounge and spotted Abe Vigoda. (If you were born before 1970 or watch TV Land, you know him as "Fish.") I qualified on both counts, plus I sold the *Barney Miller* show—170 episodes worth. He was sitting on the sofa staring at the floor, all alone in the maternity ward at Cedars Sinai. Only in LA.

Three weeks after our beautiful baby girl was born, the studio said yes to my plan for a Dallas office and we were on an airplane that afternoon. We couldn't get out of Los Angeles fast enough. Three years and another precious baby girl later, we were on our way back to Atlanta where I oversaw the studio's southeastern and southwestern regions.

We had two lovely girls, a gorgeous house, and all the toys and perks that come with a life of privilege. Life was good and we were living large. The outward appearance looked like we had made it, but I was just getting started on self-deception. The emptiness that I had learned to fill with so many material things—including a few barrels of single-malt Scotch—helped dull the pain. But my need for approval would continue to rear its ugly head, usually when my dad would visit. On one such occasion the two of us were sitting in the living room, not talking, when he caught me off guard.

"How much do you make?"

I told him I'd rather not say.

"How much?" he insisted.

"I really don't know," I said. "It's a lot."

"How much is a lot?"

"I really don't want to talk about it. It's embarrassing."

"How much?"

Here we were, sitting in a very nice house with my Porsche 911 Cabriolet parked in the driveway. My kids were in private school, and we spent money like it grew on one of the trees in our perfectly manicured back yard.

"How much?" he asked again.

"With bonuses, car allowance, profit-sharing, and benefits, our income is...." I whispered a number in his ear. It was a very big number.

"I thought it would be more than that."

He actually said that.

What did I have to do to win his approval? I was in my late thirties. I had been more successful than anyone in the history of my family. I had done more, made more, acquired more than I had ever dreamed possible. But I was still desperate for him to be proud of me. After that episode, all the deals I had made, the money, the promotions, the big houses, the toys—all the distractions I had used to deflect the pain suddenly stopped working, and I was lost.

8
Life and Death

Jesús and Lucio used what was left of the tools to dismantle the outboard motor. They retrieved several cables, some one-inch steel springs from the carburetor, and a yard-long drive shaft. Lucio twisted the springs into fish hooks and used the cables as fishing line. Salvador worked to make a spear by sharpening one end of the driveshaft on the whetstone, which took him several days. When he got tired and his hands were nearly raw, Lucio would take over. Salvador also broke off a two-foot section of the wooden molding on top of one of the dividers in the boat to make a stake, using his knife to carve a sharp point on one end. Jesús put the fishing line in the water with no bait. After two days he had not had a bite.

In early December, Salvador was standing watch, looking for boats and fish when a small fish approached the boat. He readied his driveshaft spear, which had a short piece of nylon rope attached to it so he could throw it at a fish and pull it back in. Salvador took a shot with his spear and missed. He thought he had tied the nylon rope tightly, but the spear slid through the knot and disappeared into the darkness of the ocean. He screamed at himself in frustration.

The next day, a small fish flew into the belly of the boat. Salvador sliced off five finger-length pieces of it and handed one to each man. Jesús, Lucio, and Salvador gobbled theirs down as if it were a chunk of fine sirloin. Señor Juan tried to swallow his piece, but it came back up, sending him into a fit of heaving that produced bile and blood. He had been getting weaker over the past couple of days. Only a week ago he had stood up in the boat, flexed his biceps, and declared, "I am strong!"

By Lucio's watch, it was the feast day of Our Lady of Guadalupe, the patron saint of the Americas, when another sea turtle approached the boat and Salvador went over the side to capture it. Lucio saw this as a sign that God was still with them. According to tradition, this was a day to reflect on issues of faith and ask God for greater understanding. The men enjoyed their turtle feast and decided to keep track of the turtles they caught by scratching notches in the boat with a nail. Lucio had removed the engine cover and set it on top of the bow enclosure to use as a stove to dry out and cook meat in the sun. Barnacles continued to form on the bottom of the boat, attracting more fish, including sharks. The men used any extra turtle meat they had for bait. They probably were unaware that fish contain a small amount of Vitamin C that would help nourish their bodies.

One night in the middle of December, another storm blew in that was more violent than the one that took the fishing net. The *panga* was pushed to the top of huge swells and thrown down with incredible force into foam and darkness. Parts of the engine, the fishing hooks, some of the lines, and the engine cover were lost. In the midst of the frenzy, Señor Juan sat on the side of the boat with his legs hanging over the edge.

"Do you want to die?" Jesús yelled at him. Señor Juan ignored him.

"You are making the ocean angry!" Jesús said. "Stop it!"

Over the next few days Señor Juan began to suffer from delusions, and Salvador prayed for him. Farsero mostly sat by himself and cried. Lucio's ears started bleeding from an infection. Señor Juan and Lucio wrapped themselves in blankets and huddled under the bow covering while Salvador prayed and read his Bible. Salvador occasionally attempted to engage the others in reading it as well. For now they had food, hydration from the turtle blood, and water from intermittent rainfall.

By Christmas the fishermen were a thousand miles from San Blas. Back home, Lucio's grandmother decorated her table and set a place for Lucio. She had set a place for Lucio at dinner ever since he was considered missing. She prayed for Lucio's safe return twice a day in front of the picture of the Virgin Mary that served as the focal point of her homemade altar. Every day, she would read the Tuesday prayer from her tattered prayer book because the last time she saw Lucio was on a Tuesday:

O Lord God omnipotent, I beseech Thee by the Precious Blood of Thy divine Son Jesus that was shed in His bitter crowning with thorns, deliver the souls in purgatory, and among them all, particularly that soul which is in the greatest need of our prayers, in order that it may not long be delayed in praising Thee in Thy glory and blessing Thee forever.

Against his grandmother's wishes, some family members organized a memorial service for Lucio, which she refused to attend.

"He is alive," she continued to insist. "I know it. My mother told me in a vision." She swore that her mother, who died several years ago, often spoke to her in dreams. "She came to me and told me he is on the sea with other men. I asked her when I could have him back and she told me, 'Not yet, but soon.'"

Lucio had been bleeding from his ears for eight days. Salvador told him he must pray to God and ask for healing. Exhausted, Lucio finally gave in and began to pray. Señor Juan was now incoherent most of the time, and Salvador pleaded with him to eat something.

"*Juanito*, you can't survive if you don't eat," he said. "Tell me what you want and I will catch it and dry it out for you in the sun."

"I have all the best cereals at home," Señor Juan said, staring out at the water.

"We are not at home, Juanito. If you don't eat, you will die."

"I can't do it," said Señor Juan. "It's disgusting, and I will only throw up again." His mood turned somber. "I really messed up didn't I? I got us all in trouble."

"It's okay," said Salvador. "But you have to eat."

"I'll take two pairs of sandals," Señor Juan shouted to no one in particular. "One pair for me and one pair for my mother." Salvador quietly backed away, leaving his companion alone with his delusions.

Over the next ten days, Señor Juan deteriorated rapidly, vomiting blood all over himself and relieving himself where he sat. Salvador and Jesús tried to make him as comfortable as possible, brushing his teeth, rinsing his mouth, washing his face, cleaning him. When he wasn't yelling out or muttering bizarre statements, Señor Juan moaned in agony. Finally, his eyes rolled back into his skull and his tongue hung out. Salvador was fishing when he heard the shout.

"What is it, *hermano*?" Salvador asked, moving in close. Señor Juan did not answer. The commotion woke Jesús.

"Is he alive?"

"No," Salvador said softly. "He is dead."

Jesús started to cry. The prospect of death was now a reality. The men undressed Señor Juan and washed him clean. Hours later, the body stiffened with rigor mortis. They decided to keep the body on the boat for a few days in hopes of rescue and a proper burial.

Conditions in the middle of the Pacific can reduce a dead body to bones in nine days, experts say. Without oxygen flowing through the body, tissues and cells break down, releasing fluids and gases that create pressure within the body, causing it to inflate as the fluids move into body cavities. After only a few days, the fluids and gases leak out and the body collapses; the skin develops a creamy consistency, begins to turn black, and smells of decay.

Three days after Señor Juan died, the men were overcome by the smell and had to bury him at sea. Farsero sat by himself crying while the other men lifted the body to the top of the bow enclosure. Salvador placed a rosary around Señor Juan's neck. He said seven prayers before they threw the body overboard. As they did, a piece of skin from the body came off in Lucio's hand. He shuddered and threw it in the water, and they watched the body float away.

9
Lost

Facing my colleagues each day had become nearly impossible, and my doctor suggested I might be suffering from Generalized Anxiety Disorder. Whenever I was under pressure, my body released massive amounts of adrenaline, increasing my breathing and heart rate—a classic fight-or-flight response. The good news, he said, was that it was treatable. The bad news was that I was always under pressure. Anxiety was part of my job description. My industry demanded my performance—no matter what.

I left the doctor's office with a prescription for Xanax in hand. I got it filled right away and took one. It helped, so I took more. I had to fly to Dallas to complete a deal a 44-year-old colleague had been working on when he suffered a stroke (he made a full recovery). After a few days, I called the doctor to say that I was out of pills and that the dosage had barely taken the edge off. He was horrified. He had given me a month's supply, enough to get a grieving widow through her husband's funeral and beyond. My prescription couldn't even get me out of Texas.

Around that time, I went to Iowa to meet Pee-Wee for a weekend of golf. While we were out on the course, he casually told me that a couple of months earlier he had become so depressed that he considered buying a pistol at a pawn shop. He said he was now taking Prozac, and it was helping. This guy was one of the happiest, most entertaining guys on the face of the earth. He was on Prozac? It sounded like a bad joke. In the Crown Room at O'Hare before boarding my plane back to Atlanta, I surfed the Web for information about depression and took a ten-question quiz. I answered yes to every one.

At the risk of sounding like one of those needy, self-diagnosing guys with too much time on his hands, I broached the subject with my doctor when I got home. I told him about my friend and how I had aced the depression quiz. He thought I might be on to something so he prescribed an antidepressant to go with the anxiety medication.

It was a rough year. Depression was getting the better of me, and anxiety was munching on the leftovers. I tried everything: Celexa, Buspar, Effexor, Zoloft, Paxil, Lexapro, Wellbutrin, and Trazadon, each with a nasty little helping of side effects all its own. As if walking around sweaty, shaky, and paranoid weren't enough, I had dry mouth, diarrhea, insomnia, and the list goes on.

On my next visit to the doctor, I tossed out an idea.

"I think I need to stop drinking." I said.

"What makes you say that?"

"Well, I've been noticing that whenever I drink alcohol with my medication, I fall down a lot." On a typical Saturday, I would get up, pop open a beer around 10 a.m., and keep on drinking until I went to bed.

We agreed that I should cut back, and I left with a prescription to counter the effects of alcohol just in case I couldn't stop on my own, which I couldn't. (Quitting turned out to be a lot harder than just deciding to quit.) He also put me in touch with a local psychiatrist who recommended a twelve-step program. My life was becoming a made-for-TV movie. So I agreed to go. For a while I just sat back and listened, but attending the meetings became another buoy that kept me afloat. I did ninety meetings in ninety days. I haven't had a drop since. At the time, stopping the drinking seemed like the answer to all my problems.

But it wasn't. Life at the studio got worse. I was in a downward spiral, and no matter how hard I tried I couldn't pull out of it. After fourteen years on the job, I was being treated like an intern, and I began to retreat and get defensive. I could not perform and people noticed. It was terrible—it seemed as if everyone was waiting for me to screw up big. I was humiliated but defiant, despite the advice I had been given to lie low and wait out the storm. There probably were people trying to help me out of the fog, but if there were, I didn't notice them. A few months later, I was summarily dismissed, after which I felt strangely relieved. At least I didn't have to pretend anymore. I made plans to take some time off, but before I could really get my feet up, a friend called with an idea that piqued my interest. He had a business associate who had founded an Internet company in the late nineties and was both a billionaire and a great guy. He owned an interest in a little company called HowStuffWorks, an online encyclopedia of sorts. He envisioned a television show based on this concept, with an edgy entertainment angle, and my friend thought I was the guy to make it happen.

Without giving it much thought, I hopped on board in early spring 2002 and was eventually asked to run the company, which was losing money at the time. I flew up to their headquarters in Cary, North Carolina, every week and continued to go to AA meetings. Things were okay but not great, and the meds seemed to be helping. I had quit drinking, but I started smoking again and got hooked right away. I was able to help move HowStuff-Works from losing money to breaking even, though it probably would have happened anyway because they had great content. I had been there about two years when I started to stall, and so did the company. I couldn't focus again, couldn't remember things. My anxiety came back with a vengeance, and so did the depression. My doctor upped the dosage on both medications, which seemed to be all I had to fight it.

Around Christmas of that year, I was having lunch with some friends when I got a call from Carmen. The security company that monitored our house had just called her. Something had set off the smoke alarm in the garage, and the fire department had been dispatched. I shrugged it off and told her to call me back if there was a real fire. She did, and there was. As I turned onto my street, I saw several fire trucks in front of the house and plumes of black smoke billowing from the second-story windows. Some of the firefighters were reeling in the hoses; they had already put out the flames. Carmen was talking to the battalion chief about what might have caused the fire. Apparently, our housekeeper had dumped the fireplace ashes into a trash can in the garage, unaware that the embers were still hot. The entire garage and attic above were destroyed.

I listened intently to the fireman for a few minutes, looked at the mess in front of me, and decided to mow the lawn. Now that might sound strange. All I can say is that it seemed like a good idea at the time. I love to cut grass. I could do it all day long. Someday, I'd like to spend most of my time cutting grass on a tractor on a farm so large I could start mowing at one end on Monday and not reach the other end until Sunday. And when I finished, it would be time to start all over. A wise man once told me that the reason some men love to cut grass is that it gives them a sense of instant accomplishment that requires little brainpower. You just put the wheel on the line where you just mowed and go. When you're done, you can sit on the porch, crack a beer, and admire your work. Nobody yelling at you. It's virtually idiot-proof.

Picture the scene: My garage is smoldering, and the firemen are rolling up the hoses. Joe is cutting the grass. Maybe I felt left out of the action. Plus, on the way home I had chewed up several anxiety pills, fearing that what I was about to see wasn't going to be good. I guess I figured I could at least make the yard look nice, seeing as how Christmas was just around the corner.

With our house uninhabitable, I insisted that we check into the Ritz-Carlton to spend the holidays. Carmen went about the post-fire cleanup, and I acted as if nothing were amiss. I was no help to her because, frankly, I liked living at the Ritz. It was a luxurious way to suspend reality, a life-size Xanax complete with room service and cozy European-style down duvets. Despite the plush accommodations, I needed more to fight off reality. I took whatever pills I could get my hands on and grew darker with each passing day.

A few weeks later, I decided to make a trip to south Texas to visit my dad, a trip that in my imagination held the promise of change, possibly even a breakthrough. I told him I was coming to play golf and get some sun. But I went because I wanted answers. *Was my depression hereditary?* I was positive I had once heard my dad mention something about being depressed. I needed to know. I was desperate.

I headed to Brownsville where my father spent a few months each winter. The first night we went across the border to have dinner in Mexico. After we finished eating, I took a breath, confessed to my father that I was suffering from depression, and asked him how he had been able to deal with it so long ago.

"I've never had any problem with any of that," he said, looking me straight in the eye. "I turned 40 once, too. You'll get over it."

I couldn't believe what I had just heard. This wasn't about turning 40. How could my own father trivialize my pain and desperation? I couldn't believe he refused to admit what I knew he had said years earlier. I couldn't believe my dad would lie to me. Most of all, I couldn't believe I had expected my father to be any different than he had always been. But it still hurt.

I walked across the street to a little gift shop with a flashing "*Farmacia*" sign in the window. I was ready to kill the pain even if it killed me in the process. I bought as much as they would sell me: Vicodin, Valium, and more Xanax. I spent the rest of the weekend buying drugs in buckets, taking as much as I could and stuffing the rest in my golf bag. Out of my mind on prescription meds on the way home, I missed my connecting flight in Houston. Blocks of time were disappearing.

Back in Atlanta, the downward spiral continued. The pills had become like alcohol to me, only worse. But I didn't feel as guilty because I thought of them as part of my "medical" treatment. I took pills in the morning, and by the time I got to work I was ready for another round. By dinnertime I was ready for more pills and the dark comfort of my bed. I would sleep fourteen hours, then start the process all over the next morning. I was the walking dead.

10

Choosing Life

Farsero cried for days after Señor Juan's funeral. He wouldn't crawl under the bow cover to get out of the sun. His skin was bubbled and peeling. Then he stopped crying. One morning Farsero didn't wake up. "That is the best death to have," Lucio said. "To die while you are dreaming."

Just as they had done for Señor Juan, they kept Farsero's body on board for three days, praying that a ship would come so he could have a decent burial. Finally, the stench became unbearable. Farsero's service was similar to Señor Juan's, except that this time each of the men read a passage from the Bible. That night Salvador secretly offered God a simple deal: "Dear God," he prayed, "I will give my life if you will allow my friends to live. Amen."

In mid-February it started to rain heavily. Once the gas containers were full, each of the men was able to take a bath in the rainwater that had collected in the bottom of the *panga*. They had not eaten for two weeks, even though the waters were full of food. None of the men wanted to risk becoming a tiger shark's next meal. The sharks were small but ferocious enough to easily bite off an arm. Late one afternoon Salvador and Jesús were fishing and saw a five-foot shark just off the side of the boat. Salvador grabbed the wooden stake and plunged it into the head of the shark from the front. The angle of the impalement prevented the shark from diving or pulling away to free itself.

"Hold this and don't let it get away!" Salvador shouted to Jesús, handing him the stake. Salvador stood up and ripped off his shirt. "The knife!" he yelled to Lucio, motioning to the tools. Lucio gave a shark knife to Salvador, who bit down on it and jumped into the bloody water. He grabbed the shark with both hands, one on each side fin, while the shark thrashed violently back and forth. Salvador slowly gained control of the shark, turning it as if he were steering a jet-ski, trying to wear the shark down. Jesús hung on to the side of the boat and gained some leverage to jam the stake deeper into the hard muscle of the shark's head. Salvador steadied the animal and prepared to let go of the right fin and take the knife out of his mouth when the shark thrashed wildly. Having released the fin to grab the knife, Salvador was losing the battle and tiring quickly, trying his best to keep his head above the surface of the foam and blood.

"More sharks!" Lucio screamed when he spotted several more tigers approaching rapidly. Salvador's head was under the murky water and he could not hear the warning or see anything. He kicked his legs and lifted his head toward the fin, locking his teeth on it and biting down as hard as he could. Instantly, he felt a burning pain in his mouth from the tiny thorn-like denticles that covered the shark's fin. He raised the knife over his head and with all of his strength tried to drive it into the side of the shark, but the blade bounced off as if it had hit solid steel. Salvador raised the knife again, this time plunging it into the shark's eye. The tiger went limp. Lucio and Jesús lifted the shark into the boat and then pulled Salvador out of the water. The shark was still snapping its jaws when Lucio grabbed the knife and twisted it deeper into the creature's brain.

Salvador's lip was split and two of his teeth were loose. His chest was badly scratched and bleeding, but he was smiling. Today was his birthday. The three men devoured the shark—brain, eyes, stomach, and all its contents. Lucio and Jesús reserved the heart and liver for Salvador and insisted he take them. When the men had finished eating, they sliced the remaining meat into steaks, rinsed them in saltwater, and laid them out on the bow to dry.

In March the rain came almost every day. Turtles and birds were plentiful, and there was a seemingly endless supply of fish. Thanks to their protein-rich diet, their need to hang off the back of the boat and discharge their solid waste now occurred only every other week. By April they were nearing the Pacific shipping lanes and counted more than a dozen large vessels in the distance, still too far off to see the *panga*. Lucio kept track by cutting notches in the side of the boat. They invented games to pass the time, one of which was "What Will You Have for Dinner?" They would imagine that the meat they were eating was a piece of hot bread or a favorite fruit, vegetable, or dessert.

"A cheeseburger and a Coke," Salvador would often say, "with chocolate cake and vanilla ice cream." Lucio's favorite was banana bread.

"Can you remember how it smells when it's fresh?" Jesús would ask him.

"I can smell cigarettes and pancakes!" shouted Lucio one day. "Just like they are here in the boat!"

Jesús often thought about Jocelyn and little Juanchillo back home and wondered why this was happening to him. He had not been the best of husbands. He knew he had often been cruel to Jocelyn, treating her more like a servant than a wife. Just before he left for San Blas, he had searched in vain for some money he had hidden away. He yelled at Jocelyn for moving things around. He later found the money in the pocket of his pants but did not apologize. He frequently made her get out of bed when he came home after a night of drinking with his pals, demanding that she make something for him to eat. She was only 16 when she got pregnant and barely 20 now. He knew she was at home with no money and no idea of what had happened to him. He pictured her working herself to exhaustion trying to raise his son alone. He vowed to God that if he survived this ordeal, he would be a better husband and father. He also vowed to quit drinking. He knew that Jocelyn would be giving birth any day now, and the thought of it brought him to tears.

"Crybaby!" teased Lucio, who was in a dour mood himself. "Are you not a man?"

"I *am* a man!" Jesús shot back. "But men cry, too. I cry because of my family. You don't cry because you have no one."

"I was born just as you," said Lucio. "I have my mother, my father, my grandmother!"

"No," Jesús insisted. "You have no one!"

Salvador had had enough.

"Calm down!" he shouted. "Don't be stupid. We need each other." He ordered them to different parts of the boat where they remained silent until Lucio finally spoke.

"I'm sorry, Jesús. I shouldn't have said those things to you. It's just the hopelessness."

"God will look over us," Salvador assured them. "He will protect us. We have food and water, and we are friends. God wants us to be friends." Jesús and Lucio rarely argued after that. From time to time, Lucio trimmed the other men's hair and beards with a shark knife.

On cold nights they would sleep three in a row under the bow enclosure to keep warm. Lying together in close quarters, they would speculate on where they were and where they might end up. Jesús thought Hawaii; Salvador thought China. Lucio had no opinion. Whenever an airplane passed overhead, they would try to guess where it was going. Salvador knew they could not get back to where they started because of the currents. Wherever they were headed, he said, they should try to get there faster.

So they went to work fashioning a mast out of the wooden trim on two of the dividers and hoisted a pair of blankets as sails. This did not increase their speed much, but the activity gave them a feeling of accomplishment and they felt a bit more in control. Soon after, a storm took the sails and nearly capsized the boat. Through May and June they stuck with the routine: fish, sleep, eat.

During that time, the *panga* passed by several islands—
Christmas, Fanning, Baker—but never got near enough
for anyone to see them.

By July, the fishermen were facing greater challenges
than the heat: Jesús was having severe stomach pains and
Lucio's vision was failing, as was Salvador's. Their energy
levels were dangerously low, and they were moving much
more slowly. The end was near, and they knew it.

"I do not fear death," Salvador told his companions.
"Not when I am with you."

11

Choosing Death

Shortly after my visit with my dad, Carmen and I went to dinner with our friends Howard and Mary. Back in my drinking days, Howard and I had become good friends. We did guy stuff together—playing golf and tennis, smoking cigars, attending sporting events, going to movies our wives wouldn't go see, and, of course, cocktailing. I never noticed he was only having one drink to my ten. One day we were playing golf, and I was egging him on.

"You should drink more," I blurted out after I hit a long four-iron two feet from the flagstick. (I always thought I played better when I was a little tipsy.)

"I am perfectly fine with the amount I drink," he said.

What an odd thing to say, I thought to myself. I'm sure I was suppressing an inner voice that was telling me, *Hey, doofus, you should take a lesson from this guy—he has his life together.* The next time we played golf I was able to tell him that I hadn't had a drink in 43 days. I didn't mention the medications.

Several times during the dinner, I got up to use the restroom and Howard had to keep me from falling down. It was so uncomfortable for Carmen. And so sad. No one knew what to do or say. I, of course, was oblivious. The next morning, Howard asked me to join him for tennis, and I took great pains to sufficiently medicate so I wouldn't feel the weight of his judgment—or anything else for that matter. After I had missed most of the balls he hit to me, he was fed up. We left the court, walked over to the pond, and sat down. He had never looked so serious with me. In my mind, we were "guy" friends, and guy friends usually don't want to mess things up by getting serious. Guy friends usually sit back and watch their buddy implode—"It's none of my business...He's just going through a hard time...He'll be fine." Not Howard. He wasn't about to show up at my funeral and kick himself for not doing something before it was too late.

"Joe, you have got to get help. You are not the same Joe that we used to know. You need to go someplace and get whatever it is that's messing you up off your chest."

"Okay," I said immediately.

Now Carmen had been saying the same thing for months, but for some reason I couldn't hear it from her. I told Howard I would get help—soon. But first there was a breakfast meeting I had to get through with some investors who wanted me to be part of their latest project. The next morning, they were waiting expectantly at the Ritz-Carlton for the guy who had been described as "the perfect fit," the guy who "had it all together." That guy never showed up. But I did.

I pulled into the valet line having taken several Xanax tablets and a couple of Vicodin pills from my new Mexican stockpile, just to make sure. I had also elected to double-down on a new anxiety drug my doctor thought might help. Suffice it to say that I was in even rarer form than usual. I got out of my Porsche, handed the keys to the valet, and walked in, completely out of my mind and certainly not ready for prime time. When I sat down, I started to feel the cumulative effects of the pills. I could feel panic coming on, but the great thing about Xanax is that as soon as you feel a twinge of anxiety, you take one and the anxiety is whisked away and wrapped in a yummy cream-puff. No matter how intense the situation, you somehow feel as if everything is just peachy.

So I thought I could handle it. With pharmaceuticals on my side, I was ready to take command, to be the executive I once was. But the new anxiety drug sent me over the top—put me under the table, actually. By the time I ordered my fruit plate, I was slurring, bobbing, and occasionally nodding off. But the yummy Xanax cream puff did its job. It made me think I had pulled it off without a hitch.

When I got home, I doubled over with the flu and began a 36-hour cycle of vomiting and diarrhea during which everything that could be expelled from my body was. I was the "sickness" part of the "in sickness and in health" vow made flesh, and Carmen was forced to contend with sights and smells no human being should ever have to contend with—or clean up after. When it was over, I had a moment of clarity. I was empty—and it felt terrible. But at least I could feel enough to see through the fog.

Carmen found the stash of medications I had bought in Mexico and confronted me. Busted. She called my psychiatrist and told him what was going on, then I got on the phone and told him I was quitting the antidepressants and anxiety meds cold turkey. He advised me not to do it. I didn't care. I couldn't live like this any longer. If I needed to take pills to keep me going, then I would just as soon die.

He insisted that I see him the next day. I had spent the night before researching treatment facilities. There were some out west that promised good results along with resort-style accommodations, spa treatments, and beautiful scenery—a Ritz-Carlton for the depressed. It sounded awesome. After all, I didn't want to be with the regular depressed people—I had "designer depression." Beating it was going to take intensive outpatient therapy, 400-thread-count sheets, and an on-call massage therapist. The doctor, however, thought that spending $50,000 a month in Arizona didn't make sense when there were programs just as good in Atlanta. Fine. At least I would be able to sleep in my own bed and spend time with my family. He booked an appointment for me for Monday.

As soon as I left his office, I started to worry about the possible ramifications: *Was this going to get me fired? What would our friends think? What about my stock options?* Surely my boss and the rest of the folks at work would want me out. On the way home, I took inventory of the what-ifs and decided I was probably going to get canned. Almost in tears, I called my attorney, who told me how I should approach my colleagues, and—if I needed to down the road—how to file a disability claim. Next, I called my closest friends to tell them I was checking into a hospital for depression. Every one of these conversations started and ended in tears. I was never so publicly humiliated. I had failed at life. I was no longer a guy who could figure things out on his own. I was broken.

I spent the rest of the week prepping for my treatment—there were lots of details to consider, the last of which included calling my office. I started with my boss but couldn't track him down, trading urgent messages and emails with his secretary until I got him at his beach house in Miami. I was very nervous, expecting to hear something like, *We can't help you. We can't give you the time off. This is your problem. Don't let the door hit you on the way out.* Instead, he met me with grace and understanding, this billionaire on Fisher Island who could have easily spent ten times my net worth finding a replacement without giving it a second thought.

"You do whatever you need to do and take whatever time you need to get yourself well," he said. "We'll take care of everything around here until you get back." I hung up the phone and cried.

The next morning, I woke up with the familiar pain, fear, and uneasiness. Around ten, I got a call from Joshua, a close friend who wanted to meet for iced tea. Carmen and Joshua's wife, Allison, were having a garage sale, and the artifacts from my studio days were going like hotcakes. It was raining, and I was sitting in a lawn chair, tearing up as I watched *Seinfeld* posters and other memorabilia go for next to nothing—trophies from days gone by, proof that I once had been capable of great things.

Joshua came by and drove me to a restaurant, opting for a table in the back. Our iced teas came, and Joshua threw his Bible on the table. He didn't say anything for a while; he just listened to me talk about my fears about the psychiatric hospital. After about ten minutes, he leaned in close.

"Look," he said. "I'm sure the doctors will have all kinds of great stuff to tell you about why you're depressed. I'm sure you probably have some sort of chemical imbalance." He shifted in his seat before going on. "I don't want you to go into this thinking that some psychobabble and some drugs are going to fix you for good. There's only one lasting solution for your problem—and that is a *relationship* with God."

Now I had been to church. I went to Mass with Carmen and the girls, even taught some Sunday School, and God was all over the twelve-step programs I had been attending for the last few years. But, I didn't know anything about a relationship with God, and I didn't understand what that had to do with my addiction and depression anyway. Still, I agreed to pray with Joshua right there at the table. And an amazing thing happened. It wasn't like any other prayer I had ever heard or pretended to pray. It was like one of those Southern Bible Belt, come-to-Jesus prayers, the kind where you call out for God's help knowing full well that if he doesn't show up, you're doomed. I had never met Jesus—probably wouldn't know him if I saw him—but praying this way felt natural and real. I was flinging my heart out over iced tea. When we finished praying, we were both in tears. That night I crawled under the covers, hoping my iced-tea prayer would take.

When I woke up the next morning, I was terrified. I had quit the painkillers cold turkey. For the first time in a long time, I felt it all—the emotional anguish, the throbbing grief, the physical pain. Everywhere I looked there was doom and dread. It felt as if someone had sucker-punched me in the stomach, then delivered the worst possible news a person could hear—you've been fired, you're going to jail, your wife is leaving you, *and* your daughter has been kidnapped by a child molester. And, by the way, the IRS is holding for you on Line One.

Truthfully, I was hoping for something more, especially considering Joshua's prayer the day before. Now that all the toxins had left my body and I was thinking clearly, I began to wonder if change would ever come. After forty-two years of trying to save myself, what was one prayer going to do? How I wished there was hope in a God who could rescue me, even if it was just from the pain of living. I had tried every other option. Joshua had almost challenged God yesterday. In essence, he said, "God, if you don't come right now to this man, he is going to die." And I believed him.

That Saturday, February 14, was cold, and I was moving slowly. I don't remember a lot, except that I never really got dressed. I put on sweatpants and bedroom slippers and my bomber jacket with the *Seinfeld* logo on the back because as long as you've got a cool jacket you're not a loser, right? Carmen was still working the garage sale, and I showed up looking like I had just escaped from a psych ward. *Happy Valentine's Day, honey! Say, would you mind doing me a favor this year and drop me off at the loony bin?*

I parked myself in a lawn chair in the rain and tried not to cry. Allison sometimes reminds me how pitiful, afraid, and sad I looked, and how she and Joshua would pray that I could hang on for one more day. Carmen must have been praying, too, and she must have been scared to death. Allison stared at me in that lawn chair for the longest time, trying to will me back to wholeness. I'm sure I didn't even notice.

12

Rescue

August 9, 2006—PACIFIC OCEAN

Jesús, Salvador, and Lucio were drifting in the western Pacific, roughly 6,000 miles from where they had started 286 days earlier. They were somewhere among the Marshall Islands off the coast of Australia. They had killed and eaten 108 sea turtles. They had seen 25 ships. Two crew members were dead, and Lucio was near death himself. As they huddled together like sardines under the bow enclosure, Salvador felt a thump on the side of the boat. Sharks and whales had thumped the boat on many occasions, but this thump was different. He also noticed a humming noise.

"Is that the wind?" asked Lucio.

Salvador pulled himself up by the side of the boat and covered his eyes as he squinted into the afternoon sun. He thought he was seeing a mirage.

"Jesús! Lucio!" he shouted. "We are saved!"

"Leave us alone," moaned Lucio. "Let us sleep,"

"No, look!" Salvador yelled, pointing. Jesús and Lucio crawled from under the bow enclosure and saw several Asian men pulling alongside them in a small boat, with a gigantic trawler as a backdrop. Registered in Taiwan, the Koos 102 is half the size of a football field, with a predominantly Chinese crew. (The Taiwanese papers were the first to report the story, hailing it as a 21st century "Robinson Crusoe" adventure.)

Jesús, Salvador, and Lucio cried tears of joy and embraced each other, thanking God for their rescue. They were helped into the small rescue boat and then taken to the trawler. The three fishermen huddled together in one spot while the crew carefully hoisted the *panga* on board. The rescuers seemed more concerned about the *panga* than they were about the survivors. Jesús, Salvador, and Lucio were restless during their first few nights aboard the ship, tormented by nightmares and the fear that their rescue was just a dream. It took them many days before they could accept the reality that they were safe.

The Koos 102 had picked up the three fishermen on its way out to sea on a tuna-fishing expedition, which meant they would be staying at sea for several more weeks until their cargo hold was full. The crew told the fishermen to stay indoors in an air-conditioned cabin. Initially, they were fed only soup and fresh water. When processed foods containing preservatives were added to their diet, the three fishermen got sick and their limbs began to swell. After several days of rest, they were summoned to the captain's quarters to meet Yeng Ching Shui, who did not speak Spanish. The fishermen, of course, did not speak Chinese. The captain pointed to a map of the area islands, attempting to learn which island the men had come from. The men were confused. They had never seen these islands on a map before. The fishermen kept shaking their heads "no." They realized they somehow had to explain to the captain that they were not from the local islands. They kept stepping back from the map and repeating, "Mexico." Finally, after five attempts, the captain got it. He shook his head as if to say, "Impossible."

The trawler continued to operate as usual with their three guests aboard, staying at sea for two more weeks. Once communications were established with the mainland, the lines started buzzing between the ship, the port, the Mexican authorities, the families of the men, and the owner of the fishing company, who ordered the ship back to Majuro, the capital of the Marshall Islands. When the manager of the port was asked how the fishermen looked when he met them, he said, "A little skinny and exhausted—and understandably so. By the time I saw them on the docks they were in pretty good condition, but that was two weeks later."

During their time aboard, the Koos 102, Jesús, Salvador, and Lucio gained strength each day, gradually adding more substantial food to their diet. They slept well and often and enjoyed long showers, trying their best to wash away nine months at sea. They trimmed their hair and nails. And they continued to read the Bible. The first time they sat down with the crew in the dining area, they were served a special meal: sushi. As the plates were set in front of them, the survivors looked at each other in disbelief.

"They *are* going to cook this, *aren't they?*" Jesús whispered to Salvador.

"I don't think so."

"What should we do?" asked Jesús through clenched teeth.

"Smile and eat it," said Salvador.

Lucio shook his head and shoved a piece of raw fish into his mouth. Jesús and Salvador did the same.

Meanwhile, the Mexican government was working on a plan to get the men back to Mexico. All the men had when they were rescued were the scraps of clothes on their backs, a few tools, and Salvador's Bible. An official was dispatched from the Mexican Embassy in New Zealand, which was the closest one to Majuro, to establish passports and help the men reconnect with their families.

The story of the fishermen hit the news wires on August 16, but in the United States it got lost among some of the day's other headlines:

—*Bomb Threat Closes Port of Seattle Terminal 18*

—*Coast Guard Arrests Drug Kingpin Javier Felix in California Gulf*

—*Russian Patrol Boat Fires on Japanese Fishing Boat, Killing 1*

—*United Airlines Flight 923 Makes Emergency Landing in Boston*

—*Volcano Erupts in Ecuador, Spewing Four-Mile Cloud of Ash*

—*Ford to Shut Down 10 North American Plants, Cut Production 21 percent*

—*International Astronomy Union No Longer Recognizes Pluto as Planet*

And the big one:

—*John Mark Karr Arrested in Bangkok for Murder of JonBenet Ramsey*

As the Koos 102 approached Majuro, several boats came to meet her about an hour from port. The press had gotten wind of the story. Virtually every major media outlet sent a reporter to the tiny island to greet the survivors. The men spent almost a week in Majuro waiting for the Mexican authorities to prepare their passports. Fittingly, their first meal back on land was a cheeseburger and a Coke, with chocolate cake and vanilla ice cream for dessert.

13
Found

I remember only two things about Sunday, February 15, 2004. The first is kneeling in church, reading the prayer at the back of the Missal and questioning why God would allow me to live, if this was what my life was to be—never-ending fear and doom. The other thing I remember is looking at the clock around six that evening, knowing I had an appointment at the Cuckoo's Nest the next morning and not caring. I was finished. All I was thinking as I crawled into bed was, *Please, just let me die.*

I had a rude awakening after midnight, like someone had shoved smelling salts up my nose to jolt me back to consciousness. I didn't know where I was. My clothes were drenched. I found a pair of dry underwear in the closet, put them on, and crawled back in bed. I closed my eyes and lay in the stillness. Then it came, amid the darkness and failure and uncertainty, the most amazing peace. It was a feeling of lightness like nothing I had ever experienced. Peace. Contentment. Assurance. All three came in a trickle at first, then a rush, as if my heart were a bucket and hope was being poured into it—a my-cup-runneth-over kind of thing. I had no fear that it would wear off, nor could I do anything to make it stay. The pain was gone—every ounce of it. The knot in my neck and shoulders, gone; the burning in the pit of my twisted stomach, gone; the lump in my throat, gone; the fear, gone.

I woke up Carmen, who, given the cloud of illness encircling our home over the last week, probably thought I was about to throw up. Or maybe that I was giving her a two-minute warning about a swarm of locusts that was on the way, her husband having become the oracle of bad news and plagues.

"Honey, wake up. Something has happened," I announced as I shook Carmen's shoulder.

"What? What is it?" she said, barely awake.

"I think God has just come into my life," I said, not knowing exactly what I meant by this. Carmen wasn't sure, either. I had gone to bed a vomiting, sweatshirt-wearing failure who didn't know Jesus from Peter, Paul, and Mary. Suddenly, I'm telling her I had been paid a midnight visit by the Creator of the Universe.

"What are you talking about?" she muttered, still half asleep.

"I don't know," I said, "but everything is gone. All the pain, all my anxiety—it's gone." She looked concerned. "I'm okay," I said. "Somehow, I just know everything is going to be okay. I have this amazing peace. A joy. Like I've never felt before. It's like everything is calm and serene."

"What do you think it is?" she asked, not really expecting I had an answer.

"I have no idea," I said. "That's why I woke you up. I thought you'd know."

We sat quietly in the bed for a few minutes, still too afraid to be hopeful. But we both sensed a rescue of sorts. On the eve of my admission to a psychiatric hospital and after years of wrong turns and putting my ladder up against the wrong walls, God had shown up on a double-dare and done the unthinkable: He had saved me.

I didn't fully understand (and still don't know exactly) what happened that night. In the simplest of terms, I had surrendered, given up the life I had been barely living, not in exchange for another kind of life but because I was simply out of options. That night I was free-falling like a jet fighter in a death spiral when God stretched out his big supernatural safety net and caught me. It's a wonder I didn't burn a hole right through that thing.

For me, surrender was a dying breath, a whisper I couldn't hear but apparently God could. It was me finally giving up my "junk," the illusion of self-sufficiency, the belief that I had all the answers and that if I earned enough, drank enough, and spent enough, I would be "enough." When I gave up my stuff that night, it had claw marks all over it, because I had clung to it like a lovesick teenager. It was my God. Robert Downey, Jr., the actor, once described his stuff to a judge before being jailed for again violating the terms of his parole: "It's like I've got a shotgun in my mouth, with my finger on the trigger, and I like the taste of gun metal." Brother, I know how you feel.

The next morning, I was still weak, not just from being sick but because I had been subsisting for weeks on the Diet Coke-and-cigarette Happy Meal. As I stood in front of the mirror, the veil lifted and for the first time I could clearly see the physical toll. I had gone from borderline handsome to borderline homeless. I could see what had been obvious to others for so long. I had deluded myself into thinking I had game, with my fancy car and my good looks and my pharmaceuticals. That day, the truth was staring me in the face. In fact, Carmen had taken the car keys away from me before I had the chance to kill myself or some unsuspecting stranger. Seeing myself without the buffer of the junk I was holding on to was jarring, but at least I had hope. I got dressed and she drove me to my appointment.

On the way to the hospital Carmen's cell phone rang.

"Hold on, here he is," she said, passing me her phone.

"Joe, how are you doing?" the voice on the other end said. It was Kim. She and her husband, Alfred, were our first friends in Atlanta. Ironically, Carmen and Kim met when they worked at the Ridgeview Institute in 1985, the same hospital we were driving to.

"What time is your appointment?" she asked, as if she had a plan.

"10 a.m."

"Okay, we're going to start praying for you at 9:55...."

"But, Kim, something happened last night." I explained how I had felt as if I were being filled with a cool liquid and how it overflowed out of me. Then she asked me a question no one had ever asked me. I had never even heard the phrase before.

"Was it like scales falling from your eyes?"

How could she know that? How could she nail it like that?

"Yes. That's exactly what it's like!" I said with a big smile on my face.

For those of you who have never checked into a psychiatric hospital, the first order of business before admission is the all-important evaluation, the part where they decide if you're crazy enough to join their club. A few days in, I asked one of the doctors if I really needed to be there. He gave me an odd look and said, sternly, "You don't get into this place unless you really need it." I remember a nice girl taking me into a small room for the interview. My wife and doctors had already told them everything. I guess they needed to hear crazy from the horse's mouth to make it official.

"So, tell me what's been going on," she said.

I launched into it, watching her take down everything I said.

When I finished, she did a quick recap: "So, we have an episode of severe depression and anxiety combined with some abuse of medications and some past alcohol abuse. Is there anything else?" She flipped the page and her hair in one fluid motion and waited for me to respond, her eyes looking down at the sheet to make sure everything was in order. She had done this a thousand times.

I was just about cleared for takeoff, and she had to ask, "Is there anything else?" *Of course, there's something else. Only the biggest thing that had ever happened to me in my life!* But then, it was all new to me—God, serenity, even hope. I didn't know how to describe it, and I was afraid I might project the wrong kind of crazy, the kind that lands you in a straitjacket. Tears suddenly flooded my eyes.

"I think I was visited by God last night," I said softly. Her pen paused in midair. She looked up at me as if instead of God I had said Elvis.

"Really?" she said in her best nonjudgmental voice. "Why don't you tell me about that?"

I proceeded to give her a detailed account. The more I talked about it, the more I began to understand the weight of what had happened. I cried a little more. When I was done, she handed me a tissue and checked me in.

I attended the outpatient program Monday through Friday, spending the majority of time in a classroom setting. Large group discussions covered everything from the causes of depression to pharmacology to coping skills to physical fitness. Smaller groups were where we talked about our individual issues. The first day, I met my main counselor, who didn't seem like a good fit at first, mostly because he had a habit of wearing his crew neck sweater with his collar on the outside, and it bugged me. I became preoccupied with it. Maybe there was a part of me that resisted treatment—as long as I stayed hung up on some stupid detail like a shirt collar, I wouldn't have to work on getting better.

He actually turned out to be the perfect counselor. The first time we met privately, he shared a big chunk of his story, and I could relate to much of what he said. He also gave me a few pieces of scrap paper with some verses of Scripture he had jotted down. It was my first serious exposure to the Bible. A few weeks into my treatment, family members were invited in as part of the program. Carmen and I met with a family therapist, and she got what was going on right away. "Don't you see?" she asked us. "Joe's the kite, and you're holding the string." Carmen nodded. The therapist looked at her. "Wouldn't you ever like to be the kite?" Translation: *Wouldn't you like to be having fun instead of always having to be the responsible one?*

At my first group meeting I sat in one of the chairs that lined the walls of the windowless room and watched as the other patients shuffled in. They seemed like a fairly normal bunch. We each said our name and how we were feeling that day. The counselors gave us a list of words to use to describe our feelings—I guess "good," "fine," and "okay" were too pedestrian. Apparently, the approved words had a track record of cutting through the manure. I was particularly fond of "sparkly" and "fuzzy."

When everyone else had finished, the group leader turned to me and said, "So, Joe, why don't you tell us why you're here?"

I heard words come out of my mouth that had never come out of it before.

"I think I'm here to serve all of you," I said. To say this was out of character would be like saying Hannibal Lector was now a vegetarian. I don't think I had ever served anyone. I was the one who like to be served. I liked luxury hotels, and expensive sheets. And the service that came with five stars and many diamonds. I liked Carmen cleaning up the kitchen after dinner. I wasn't someone who thinks about other people's needs. I guess this was just one more layer of skin I would shed in the coming months. When I told Carmen what I said about serving the group, she thought it might have been a form of denial, like, "If I'm here to serve you people in this program, I really can't be that bad off, can I?" There may have been some truth to that.

14
Heroes and Villains

The authorities were busy making travel arrangements for the three fishermen, none of whom had ever been on an airplane. The plan was to fly them to Honolulu, then on to Los Angeles, then to Mexico City, then to their respective home cities. It was a simple plan. But somewhere between the Koos 102 and Mexico City, all hell broke loose.

When the men were rescued by the Taiwanese trawler, they never told anyone on board that they started with a crew of five, which is understandable since no one asked and no one on the trawler spoke Spanish. After some Spanish-speaking people showed up, one of the fishermen told someone about Señor Juan and Farsero. The press jumped all over this new information and reported that the men had changed their story. Much of the coverage began to take on a sinister tone—*Did they eat their shipmates?* The press, of course, answered their own question: *They must have.*

The "heroic journey" and "amazing survival" story was replaced by rumors of cannibalism, drug-running, and conspiracy. These wild theories quickly gained traction in the Mexican press as the fishermen were traveling home. They were heroes when they left the South Pacific, but by the time they landed in Mexico City, they were villains. Murder and intrigue always sell more newspapers and deliver higher TV ratings than feel-good stories.

The press was frothing at the mouth to get to them. Before they met the press, however, the three of them were examined by a team of doctors, which only fueled speculation that the fishermen were lying. After all, the thinking went, they looked too good for guys who supposedly had been lost for more than nine months at sea. Never mind that the *Tres Pescadores* had spent two weeks resting in an air-conditioned cabin aboard the Koos 102, getting medical attention, drinking clean water, and eating rice and eventually other healthy foods. Once ashore in Majuro, the fishermen spent several days getting ready for the two-day trip to Mexico City. Nearly three weeks had passed since their rescue.

The hundred or so reporters were loaded for bear, jockeying for position in the packed conference room, eager to hear the first official words of the survivors now that they were back on Mexican soil.

Salvador, Jesús, and Lucio were all smiles when they entered the room. Camera lights flashed nonstop for a few minutes. Then the men took their seats and the questioning started.

"Are you happy to be back?"

"Yes, of course," Jesús said, leaning in to the mike.

"Did you eat the other two?" shouted one reporter.

"Are you narcotics smugglers?" yelled another.

The smiles on the faces of the fishermen vanished, and they slouched down in their chairs, stunned by the barrage of hostile questions. Their eyes were glazed, and they seemed to be staring right through the reporters. The questions continued to come rapid-fire.

"How can you prove you were fishing for sharks?"

"Why wasn't your trip registered?"

"Why didn't someone report that you were missing?"

"Why do you look so good?"

"Why aren't your nails longer?"

Salvador, Jesús, and Lucio looked like third-grade boys in English class who were being forced to watch a production of Hamlet. They heard the words, but they could not comprehend what they were hearing. These men had never faced so many questions. They were used to being told what to do.

"That is not true," Lucio responded angrily. Then he calmly spoke these words into the mike: "To people that don't believe us, well, they should hope that they never have to go through this."

"Will you take a lie detector test?" one reporter shouted.

"Yes," Jesús said without hesitation. "We have nothing to hide."

"How did you go to the bathroom?" another journalist asked.

"Just like you do," Salvador said sarcastically. The questions were now bordering on the ridiculous.

"What do you think of the presidential elections and recount?" asked a reporter.

"We followed it very closely," Jesús replied mockingly. "Newspapers were delivered to us on the boat!"

On July 2, five weeks before the rescue of the three fishermen—the *Tres Pescadores* as the Mexican press called them—Mexico had had its presidential election. The sitting president, Vicente Fox, was ineligible to run for another term. Felipe Calderon and Andres Manuel Lopez Obrador were the two main contenders. On July 6, the Federal Electoral Institute announced that Calderon had won by less than 1 percent of the vote. His opponent claimed there were polling irregularities and declared himself the winner.

It got ugly. By early August, there were angry protests in the streets—up to a million people, depending on who you believed. It was a heavyweight boxing match that had gone fifteen rounds, with each guy celebrating as if he had won and thinking that the more he acted like a winner the better his chances were of being awarded the championship belt. Both candidates had internal polling that showed them to be the winner. It was a national crisis. In July and early August, the media coverage was extensive, with reporters waiting—and presumably hoping—that the situation would explode. News stories about electoral "materials" being found in trash dumps only fueled speculation that the election had been fixed. The newspaper *Reforma* later reported that these "materials" were old photocopies that had nothing to do with the outcome. But in the news biz, a rigged election was a great story for a few weeks.

The press conference finally came to an end, and the three fishermen were ushered out of the room. They had no idea what lay ahead.

15
Living

From the outside, my life looked like a train wreck—on leave from my job, spending my days at the hospital, a wife who thought I had gone off the deep end. Almost the opposite of how things were before, when the outside looked so perfect and my insides were filled with maggots. But I had never felt so alive. The sun was brighter. Food tasted better. I was able to follow through with things. I was present with people in my life; I actually heard what they were saying. I felt connected to the world. (Right about now I suppose we should cue the Pepsi commercial.) Seriously, my addictions were gone: no compulsions, no cravings. It was—no snickering, please—a miracle. I know it sounds crazy, but it's true.

My compass had been re-calibrated. I immediately quit swearing. I wasn't consciously trying not to swear; it just didn't come out of me any longer. I started to obey all kinds of laws: crosswalk signs, speed limits. I was drawn to finding out as much as I could about God and spirituality. I picked up a book that Carmen must have put on my nightstand months ago. *The Purpose Driven Life* by Rick Warren became a textbook to me. I finished it in two days instead of the recommended forty, and reread it several times over the course of that summer. I bought the audio version and listened to it over and over.

My next-door neighbor gave me a book entitled *Half Time,* by Bob Buford, whose thesis was that life—like many sporting events—has a halftime during which we can take stock and make adjustments for the second half, focusing on significance rather than success. I was about to turn 42, roughly halfway through my life, so the message hit home.

Naturally, my daughters concluded that aliens had taken up residence in my body. They were used to the cool dad who let them watch MTV, *Saturday Night Live,* and other material completely inappropriate for teen and preteen girls. It freaked them out that I was now policing their TV and music for anything unhealthy or offensive, even TV commercials about a certain medication that might cause that legendary four-hour side-effect.

I stayed in the outpatient program for five weeks, with my boss's blessing. I soon decided that I needed a longer break, and I left that job a few weeks after I returned from my leave. I had no idea what my next move would be, but I was confident that whatever power had saved me from death was big enough to take care of us.

"What are you going to do?" someone from the group asked me before I left. "You know, for money?"

"I don't have any idea," I said, "but I'm sure God will take care of us."

"Wow! You really are in a good place, aren't you?" he said.

"Yes, I am." And I meant it.

I was officially unemployed for the first time since I was 10 years old. And I loved it. I had only one goal that summer—to not work. Of course, all kinds of people call when you don't want a job, and I got called a lot to see if I would come to work for them. I had never been good about saying no, but I was determined to find out how my life had become such a mess. I calculated our net worth and saw that we were financially secure enough to miss a paycheck or two. Those few missed paychecks would turn into several years with a lot more money going out than coming in and a 401K that would be tapped dry.

One of the requirements for discharge from the program was a written plan—you had to show them you could stay healthy on "the outside" before they turned you loose. You also had to arrange to continue therapy with an outside counselor. I would have gladly stayed a few more weeks, but my insurance ran out. When I left the program, I began to see a therapist twice a week to help me explore every dusty, cobwebbed, boarded-up corner of my heart and my mind. One day she asked me to write down everything I could remember about growing up. I had a hard time recalling many happy childhood memories, which made me angry. The therapist taught me to be patient, to let those feelings wash over me instead of trying to make them go away, which had been my customary method for handling pain.

About a week after his prayer for me, Joshua gave me a Bible, and we got together a few nights a week to try to make sense of it together. I had no idea what he was talking about most of the time. He would jump from one book to another, and I didn't understand why we didn't just read it front to back. Even so, I just felt good hanging out with him, talking about God. Joshua and I were sitting in a restaurant one night about three weeks after my "awakening" when I hunched down low across the table.

"Does everybody who knows God have this feeling? The peace? The joy?" I whispered. "And if they do, why aren't they telling other people about it—because this is unbelievable?"

"You're lucky," he said, laughing. "Stretch out in it. Most people never feel this."

When I shared my "secret" with Carmen, she was gentle with me. If I had been in her shoes, I would have said something like, "You dummy! What planet have you been living on? What do you think I've been doing the last fifteen years of our marriage?"

I went through a period of guilt and grief that summer—sad that I had missed so much of our marriage, so many important moments in the lives of my girls. Sure, we had it all, but very little of it really mattered. Why did it take me so long to notice? And how could I avoid going back there again? I prayed about these questions a lot.

I couldn't blame Carmen for being skeptical. I'm sure she was afraid that this spiritual transformation was just another one of my passing fancies, like juicing, or the South Beach Diet, or the day I decided to run a marathon even though I had never run any kind of race before, or the time I ordered a hundred boxes of green tea online because I thought it wasn't available in stores. I'm sure she must have thought I was delusional. I probably would have thought the same if she had been acting the way I was. But she gave me space, and I will be forever grateful for that. I was slowly beginning to understand the enormous sacrifices she had made throughout our marriage. She had done it all herself—not just making beds and tying hair ribbons. She had been carrying this family on her back for years, making excuses to friends for my erratic behavior, polishing up the surface of our lives that the world saw, holding in the pain I had caused. It broke my heart to think that she had, in effect, been alone for fifteen years.

I could profess complete transformation and talk about miracles all day long, but the only way I was going to convince Carmen that I had changed was show her a new man. I prayed daily for her understanding and asked God to show me His will in my life. I made a promise that if He would show me what He wanted of me, I would do it—no matter what.

One day a good friend called to say there was someone he thought I should meet, a guy who was developing family-friendly content and was looking for someone with my media experience, though I didn't know much about publishing. It sounded like a nice challenge, so we had lunch and decided to meet again in the fall, when I accepted a position in charge of distribution.

Earlier that spring, with Carmen's parents as partners, we bought a lake house, and I divided my time between the lake and home. I continued to work out and pursue God. It was the Summer of Joe, and it rocked. I finished going through the Bible for the first time and joined a men's Bible study group (they had been inviting me every other week for a couple of years). I began to reveal myself in a way I had never done before. It felt awkward, but it was incredibly freeing. Slowly, the story of the past year would dribble out until one day the study leader asked me point blank: "Tell us what happened."

I got all tight and twitchy at first, then I just let loose. Guys don't usually talk this way to other guys. Usually, our invisible force-fields detect any incoming emotions and zap them instantly. This was a different crowd, though. They welcomed it, and it really helped.

My craving for a greater knowledge and understanding of God grew, and I read nothing but the Bible for about a year. Every day. I started on page one and read all the way to the back cover, just like I was reading a regular book. One day I happened upon Ezekiel, who was a prophet who apparently could still hear from God and speak to the people of Israel even in the most difficult of times of their captivity. Chapter 22 was one of those times. As I read through it, the world he was describing in 600 B.C. sounded very much like the world today. "God looked around for someone, anyone, to stand in the gap for Him," it read, "and he couldn't find anyone, not one." At that moment, I made a commitment to God—I was going to "stand in the gap" with whatever I was going to do with my life. I wrote in the back of my Bible that if I ever formed a company, I would call it Ezekiel 22 Productions.

Then I started what some people call "church-shopping." Carmen and I had been attending a great Catholic church, she more regularly than I (she was raised Catholic), but I wanted to take in as much of God as I could. (Carmen would tell me years later how sad it made her when I wasn't sitting beside her in church.) So on Sundays,

I would attend an early service at someplace new, then pick up Carmen and the girls for Mass. One week, some friends invited us to a couples evening at a new church in town. It was in an old grocery store, and by the end of the evening, I was ready for more. So the next morning I went back. As I slid into one of the rows—not pews, the room was set up like a theater and just as dark—it felt like a concert. The service began with an incredible band playing very loud (I think I even saw smoke), and there were strobe lights. When the music ended, I fully expected to see people waving cigarette lighters over their heads. An usher passed an offering plate and told first-timers not to give anything. I thought, *Wow. This is my kind of church—rock music and no one pressuring you to give money.* Then a gigantic screen dropped down center stage and a video sermon began (the pastor was streaming live from another location). His message was awesome. I was sitting in a rock-and-roll grocery store video church—and I liked it.

16
Coincidences

The publishing company was plowing along, and I hadn't made any big plans to go anywhere. A friend who used to work on the Coke account at a large advertising agency said he had someone he wanted us to meet—a woman he attended temple with named Victoria. I didn't know it then, but my life would never be the same. Victoria's late husband had been a high-ranking executive at Coca-Cola, and before he died a year earlier, he had written a book that Victoria wanted us to publish. Victoria was tiny—five feet tall and less than a hundred pounds, but spunky.

Her late husband's book didn't seem to be a good fit for us, but she had another book idea we liked called *Dichos De Mi Madre*, "The Sayings of My Mother." It was to be a small book of about 300 Spanish sayings that would be targeted as a gift a Latino mother could give her children. Victoria was raised Jewish in Bogota, Colombia, and felt that the Latino culture in the United

States had become watered down. She saw the book as her small effort to keep her culture alive, and it would give us a point of entry into the Latino market, plus we could expand the concept to other cultures. I threw my "yes" on the pile and moved forward with the book.

Victoria had this beautiful reverence when she spoke about God. One afternoon in August, she turned to me on her way out of the office and said, "Joe, have you heard about the Mexican fishermen?"

It didn't ring a bell.

"Three Mexican fishermen were just rescued near Australia after drifting 6,000 miles for almost ten months on a tiny boat!"

I continued to stare at her. I wasn't getting it.

"They said they survived on raw fish, rainwater, and their faith in God."

I started to tune in.

"And, Joe, they had one book—a Bible—and they read it over and over."

She had my full attention now.

"I saw it on Univision last night," she said. "Look it up on the computer if you like."

I Googled it and found a three-inch article on an obscure Website and the quote about raw fish and faith.

"Isn't it an amazing story, Joe?" she asked expectantly.

I just sat there.

"Do you think you could get it, Joe?"

I was too busy to seriously consider doing anything with it, so I tried to discourage her. "Victoria, everyone will be after this story." She was undaunted.

"It would be a great story to have, Joe." She paused then said, "Can I give my nephew your information? I think he can help you with this. He lives in Mexico City. He's a lot like you, Joe, a real go-getter. He's very religious." I had never really thought of myself as a very religious go-getter.

"Sure," I said, playing along. In my mind, I had already moved on. She left the office, and I was confident I would never hear another word about the fishermen.

Carmen and I had planned to go to the lake that weekend. Summer was almost over, and we wanted one last family hurrah before the madness of another school year. We invited some friends along and planned to leave Friday around noon, so I crammed a day's worth of work into a morning and was able to wrap things up by 11:30. Just before I left, Victoria called. Her nephew Eli (pronounced EL-ee) was planning to drive from Mexico City to San Blas, the port from which the fishermen had departed. It was an 11-hour drive, but Victoria said he would be in touch when he got there.

Be in touch? I really didn't see what my role was. Had I said I was interested? Still, there was something intriguing about the story. My job with the publishing house was okay, and Carmen felt good about it. What we were doing was noble, and I was enjoying an area of media I didn't know much about. I wasn't sure if this was where God wanted me, and deep down I felt I should be doing more. I tucked the fishermen story in the back of my mind, and we headed out to the lake for the weekend.

Carmen drove, and while I was doing some work on my computer, I got a message from Eli saying he was trying to make sense of the fishermen's story and wanted to know what to say if he found any of the survivors or any family members in San Blas. As a favor to Victoria, I sent Eli some thoughts on the story. My first impression was that their story was truly miraculous—if it were true. If this was a story about faith, he should pursue that angle. Inspire people, I said. The world needed it.

The next morning we got on the boat and headed across the lake to the club pool and water slide. Carmen and I went to the gym while the kids swam. After my workout I asked a receptionist if I could use the computer. I wanted to see if there was any more news about the fishermen. The entire first page of search results was filled with headlines from all over the world. The story had taken off.

Before dinner that night, I snuck off again to go online. There were now three pages of articles. On the way home the next day, I got another email from Eli. His father had told him it was too dangerous to drive across Mexico alone. Eli wouldn't be able to make the trip. That night, Carmen approached me to confirm that I had the coming week's agenda for the girls on my calendar. This was going to be one of the six weeks a year she worked at the apparel mart, 12-hour days on her feet. But she loved it, and I was usually able to rearrange my schedule to help with carpool and meals for the girls.

"So you're still able to help me this week, right?" she asked. "I'm at the mart until Sunday." She was not expecting my response. I was not expecting my response.

"You know what, Honey? I don't think I'm going to be here for that."

She looked at me sideways. "What do you mean you aren't going to be here? We talked about this. Where are you going?"

"I think I have to go to Mexico." There was no denying it. The story that only days ago seemed so foreign and far-fetched had taken up residence in my heart. It was as if the decision had already been made and I simply walked into it.

Carmen cocked her head to the other side, squared her jaw, and knit her eyebrows together. Carmen doesn't explode, she fumes. She will clench her teeth until the enamel grinds down a few layers before she explodes. It takes a lot to get her to that point, but I know it takes even more strength for her to keep her anger stuffed down. She had many years of practice, waking up each morning wondering, "What will my husband do today?" Or "What mess am I going to have to clean up now?" I hated doing this to her, hated that for even one-second she would think that the change had worn off and that my new life had just been a fad. But I had to do it. At that moment, as much as I loved Carmen—and as much as I didn't want her to think bad things about me—my mind was made up.

"Remember the story of the Mexican fishermen I told you about?" I asked.

"What does that have to do with you?" she said, still not smiling.

"I have to go to Mexico," I said. "I think there's something to this."

She stood quietly for a few seconds, gazing at something on the wall a few inches to the left of my face. Then she fixed her eyes on me.

"Joe, be honest. Are you taking your medication?" A reasonable question, I thought, considering the hell she had been through. "Do we need to go see your doctor?"

"I'm fine. I promise. There's just something about this story. I think I have to go."

"Okaaay," she said, realizing there was no use arguing the point. "Where exactly are you going to go?"

"I don't know."

"Who are you going to see?"

"I'm not sure." I had no clue.

"Joe, how are you going to talk to anyone? You don't even know the language!" Her voice was now an octave higher. My inability to speak Spanish was the last straw.

"I haven't figured that out yet." I said.

"How long will you be gone?" Carmen's gaze returned to the same spot on the wall, perhaps buying herself a little time. I waited. I wasn't going to change my mind, but I was willing to give her the last word.

"If this is what you think you need to do, then...good luck."

It took all she had.

Carmen and I didn't talk much while I was in Mexico—sort of "Don't ask, don't tell." I thought she thought I was crazy, and I know she really didn't want to hear the details of my wild goose chase while she was back home wondering if she would ever see me again. After the first week, though, I did write her an email thanking her for allowing me the freedom to go on this journey and telling her how I felt God was with me.

I contacted the partners at the publishing company to tell them my plans. I felt that this story had the potential to be one of the greatest Mexican folktales of all time. It seemed perfect—to me. They saw it differently. It didn't fit the business model, they said. Something inside told me this wasn't about any business model. Besides, I was sure I could convince them this was the right thing for us to go after. I told them I had already bought the ticket.

When I landed in Mexico City, I called to check in at work. One of the partners told me they had discussed it, and they weren't going to be part of this. I was on my own. Not only was I on my own, I was sure they didn't want me to be part of the company any longer.

Eli picked me up in his Jeep Liberty and drove us to Polanco, a section of Mexico City something like SOHO in New York. We stopped for a bite and talked for about two hours. We connected right away—an orthodox Jew and a Christian becoming friends over a kosher meal in Mexico. After lunch, he gave me a lift back to the hotel so I could figure out what to do next. Flying to Mexico City was as far as my plan went.

I checked in at the front desk and scooped up three national newspapers from a table in the lobby. The coverage was extensive. This little story was bigger than I thought. Each paper had a front-page feature with lots of details inside. It seemed as if there was no other news—just the fishermen. Back in my room, I turned on the television to find nonstop coverage, in Spanish, of course. I sat on the end of the bed, staring at the screen.

Then I heard the word "*canabalismo.*" *Cannibalism?* I put my head in my hands and groaned. Had I come all the way to Mexico to chase down a story about man-eating fishermen? I called Eli, who said some of the authorities thought the three survivors had killed their two ship-mates for food. That was bad enough. Then he told me about the drug rumors. Maybe these guys weren't just poor fishermen who ran into some bad luck on the water, he said. They may have been on a drug run. I had to get off the phone. It was too much to take in.

Over the next hour, I tried to collect my thoughts and plot my next move. In light of these new develop-ments, there was only one realistic alternative: Go home. I thought I could come down here like some big-time in-vestigative journalist and snag the story of the century. It was crazy. The only other option would be to track down the flesh-eating drug dealers and maybe get a cookbook out of it.

I searched online again. Story after story had updates about cannibalism and drugs. It was brutal. I noticed the town of San Blas repeated in several articles. Apparently, it was where the fishermen were from. I Googled San Blas—believe it or not, this little village had a Website. There was an ad for a hotel, the Garza Canela. I sent an email asking if they had any rooms available. I went to sleep with drug-dealing cannibals on my mind.

Restless and awake at 4 a.m., I turned on my computer and much to my surprise saw a message, in English, from Josefina, a hotel manager at the Garza Canela, confirming a room for one night and one night only. They were sold out through the weekend. I figured the press and movie dealmakers had booked all the rooms. I knew if I had any hope of finding these men, I was going to need Josefina's help. I wrote back to her and emphasized that I wasn't some sleazy Hollywood producer out to serve myself and my studio. I really believed that this story would be inspiring and maybe give hope to the village of San Blas and beyond. Maybe all of Mexico. Maybe the entire world.

And then I waited. I kept checking my email and the connection to the wall. I paced the floor. By 8 a.m., I couldn't wait any longer. I called and Josefina answered. I identified myself and asked her why she hadn't responded to my message.

"I am not at the front desk right now," she said. I would find out later that San Blas was in an earlier time zone than Mexico City. I recapped my email message, and when I got to the part about hope, she cut me off.

"Oh. You need to come here," she said.

"Why do you say it like that?"

"There is no hope in San Blas. There hasn't been any hope here for a long, long time. This story is the only thing giving hope to anyone."

"How do I get there?" I asked.

"I think the road is paved coming from Puerto Vallarta," she said.

Somehow, this was not comforting.

"And from the airport?"

"You get on the road right in front of the airport and go a few hours north," she said, "When you come to a flashing yellow light, turn left and go about another hour, hour and a half, toward the coast."

"Then what?"

"That's it."

I asked her to go over the directions one more time in case I had missed anything. I hadn't. When I told her I would try to make it there by dark, she laughed.

"You must get here during the day," she said. "If you come after dark, you won't find anyone." Then she got serious. "Besides, it's very dangerous to drive through the jungle at night."

I hung up the phone, got my stuff together, and thirty minutes later I was standing at the front desk staring at a bill for 4,800 pesos. When I booked the room, I thought I was spending company money. Now that I was on my own, I felt the weight of the expense. There was going to be the airfare, a rental to drive to San Blas, my room there, plus the last-minute plane ticket I had bought to come to Mexico City, then rights fees, lawyers, agents, and who knows what else?

I couldn't even imagine what Carmen and the girls thought of me, not to mention my publishing partners, who probably saw this as one of the worst wild goose chases of all time. What was I doing? I paid the bill, and by the time I had made my way through the lobby doors, I had changed my mind again. I decided to go home and beg my wife for mercy, apologize to everyone, and forget all about the fishermen.

I got into the cab, and the doorman shut out the noise of Polanco. I stretched my legs and was about to begin crafting my apology when I heard on the radio, in English, "'Cause I gotta have faith...." The familiar notes of George Michael's song "Faith" filled the cab. *Come on!* I called Eli and filled him in on everything—the hotel, my doubts, the bill, my doubts, the song.

"Am I crazy to think this is more than a coincidence?" I asked Eli. "Is God using George Michael to tell me something?"

"Joe, there are no coincidences," Eli said. "That's what this whole thing is about, Joe, faith—the faith of the fishermen, your faith as a Christian, my faith as an orthodox Jew." He sounded confident and I believed him.

"I'm back in," I said to Eli, to myself, and to God. "I'm going to San Blas."

17
A Lamp and a Light

When I got to the Mexico City airport, the cab driver tried to collect his fare at the international departure gate, and it occurred to me that I must look like a complete gringo. He thought I was leaving the country, and he probably thought it was a good idea. Fortunately, he spoke some English and understood when I told him I needed to be taken to the domestic terminal.

"Which airline?" he asked. I had no idea.

"Which ones do you have? I need to go to Puerto Vallarta." He circled back around the airport to the domestic drop-off and helped me haul my gigantic bag out of the trunk. As he drove off, a kid approached me and motioned to my bag. Again, I'm sure it was because I looked like such a gringo.

"*No hablo Español*," I said. "I need to get to Puerto Vallarta. *Habla ingles?*"

The kid shook his head but took my luggage inside where it seemed as if there were thousands of people. I scanned the crowd for a possible English-speaking person, and when I didn't see anyone promising, I decided to check the flight monitors. There was an Aero Mexico flight leaving for Puerto Vallarta at noon. My watch said 10:50. There were some later flights, but Josefina—my closest connection to the fishermen—had warned me about driving through the jungle at night.

I looked around, hoping to find someone who might be able to help me, that nick-of-time George Burns type—you know, the TV angel God sends, the guy in the white suit, with the pack of smokes and answers? Well, he wasn't there, but I did spot a man in a pilot's uniform. Close enough.

"Excuse me," I said. "You speak English, don't you?"

"Yes."

"I'm trying to get to this little town called San Blas," I said. "Have you heard of it?" He nodded. "Is flying into Puerto Vallarta the best way to get there?"

"Mazatlan is much closer," he said with a heavy Mexican accent. "What are you going to be doing in San Blas?"

"Well," I said, "You've probably seen or read about the three fishermen who were rescued? I'm going there to try to find their families and...."

"What a hoax!" he said. I was stunned.

"What do you mean?"

"It's the government—they faked it. My father's a doctor, and he said there's no way anyone could survive that long at sea—it's impossible. He says their bodies would be destroyed. Did you see the pictures? They looked too healthy to have spent so many months on the water."

I'm sure that by this point I had gone completely white, or maybe green.

"The government has created this story to take attention away from the elections," he said as if he knew this for a fact.

Imagine that, I thought. I picked my tongue up off the ground, muttered an anemic "Thank you," and walked away. I was in a daze. He was so sure, and I was so unsure. My entire body felt as if it were split in two: one side saying, "Stick with it," the other side telling me to bag the whole thing. A guy in a uniform was telling me it was all lies. And then there was a voice on the other end of a phone line talking about hope. I ached with indecision. For some reason, I kept moving toward the Aero Mexico counter. Then I heard my disembodied voice say, "I need a ticket to Puerto Vallarta, the 12 o'clock flight, please."

The attendant looked at her screen. "There are no seats available for that flight, but I have something on the 2:30 flight that gets in to Puerto Vallarta at 4 p.m. Would you like me to book that for you?" I began to calculate. Four o'clock. That means that I could be on the road by 5 at the earliest. It probably gets dark around 6:30 or 7, but there's a one-hour time difference. The drive will take maybe four hours. I thought about Josefina again.

"I really need to be on the 12 o'clock flight, but let me think about it for a minute." Again, I thought this was it. Time to call it quits. Another roadblock, another indication that this was the end of the line. From where I stood, I could see the signs for the Delta terminal and the possibility of a flight straight home to Atlanta. It would be that easy.

"Excuse me, sir." I heard the agent say. "A first-class seat just became available for the noon flight." I asked her how much, and she said something like 5,800 pesos, which is the equivalent of about $500. *Unbelievable,* I thought to myself. *How can it be $500? I could fly to Europe for that much. Did this seat just happen to appear because of the gringo-looking "sucker" sign around my neck?* I had already spent thousands of dollars. I didn't know what to do. My job was probably gone, my kids were in private school, and I owned two homes. Was I nuts?

I stood there holding up the line, my mind racing. Then it happened. I felt this nudge, this impression, almost a voice, saying, "Joe, it's not your money. It's *My* money. Buy the ticket." I felt a weight being lifted from me as I gave the ticket agent my credit card.

"I'll take it."

I recalled a recent six-part series our church had done on money, and how none of it is ours, and how God simply lets us use it for a while. Plus, I really wanted to believe that God likes us to go first-class occasionally. The flight was boarding in fifteen minutes, so I had to hurry. As I turned to leave the counter, I saw a nun dressed in a traditional black-and-white habit standing there, a crucifix dangling from the chain around her neck. She smiled at me, knowingly.

Now maybe all nuns smile this way—maybe it's the first thing they learn in nun school—but this particular smile seemed anything but generic. It was the smile that stilled my restless soul in the middle of a crowded airport. I had chosen to find the fishermen—or, perhaps, they had chosen to find me. I wasn't sure which. I made my way through security and boarded the plane.

After I landed in Puerto Vallarta and rented a car, I found myself staring at a royal blue Ford Fiesta in the middle of a dusty parking lot. Back in the days when I was really raking in the dough, I had a Porsche—and it wasn't even that big a deal to me. I thought I deserved it. Funny how two cars that are roughly the same size can evoke such different emotions.

"Don't you have another map?" I asked the car rental agent, pointing to the local map of Puerto Vallarta that Hertz had provided. "I have to go to San Blas." I tried to hand the map back to her. "I need a map of the country."

"That's all we have," she said. "Where are you are going?"

"San Blas, north of here."

"It's easy to find." She pointed to the road between the car lot and the airport. "You take this road and keep going for three hours until you see a flashing yellow light. Turn left at the light and follow the signs." *What is the deal with the flashing lights here?*

"What if the light's not working?" I asked. It seemed like a reasonable question.

"Oh, it's working," she said, cheerfully. "It's always working."

I squeezed into the Fiesta and tried to psych myself up for the drive—a three-to-five-hour expedition through the jungle in search of flesh-eating fishermen. *Don't have a map. Don't speak the language. Don't know a soul. Great. Just great.*

I pulled out of the parking lot and onto Highway 200, thankful I could still drive a stick. A few minutes later I stopped at a convenience store to buy some Diet

Coke. When I walked in, I was immediately aware of my foreignness. This was real Mexico, not the fake, touristy, English-speaking Mexico, and it made me uneasy. A little farther down the road, I came to a security checkpoint where men with machine guns were stopping every car. *What have I gotten myself into?* I inched forward slowly until one of the armed soldiers circled the Fiesta and then tapped on my window. I rolled it down gingerly, trying to look innocent while expecting to be shot to death at any moment.

"*No hablo Español,*" I said to the soldier. I repeated the phrase in English, hoping he would understand my Midwestern accent better than my 8th-grade Spanish. Maybe he understood, or maybe I just looked too frightened to be a criminal, but after peering around the interior of the car, he waved me on. About 45 minutes into the drive, I started looking for the yellow light. Both Josefina and the Hertz lady had said it would take me several hours to reach that landmark, but I wanted to make sure I didn't miss it.

Flashing yellow light. Flashing yellow light. It became my mantra. The twisting road through the jungle was quiet except for the grinding of gears when I shifted up or down. I flipped on the radio and heard an explosion of horns, accordions, and guitars, a psychotic, cartoonish soundtrack of all my fears that nearly gave me a heart attack. I batted at the radio knob to shut it off. The noise was still ringing in my ears when I saw the machetes.

18
Angels

Sometimes talking to God can be exhausting. You pour your heart out, beg Him for something, anything, and it's almost as if He's up there in His La-Z-Boy reading the paper, nodding. And if He ever looks up, just to prove He's really listening and not just reading the comics, you can't see it. It's like being a pen pal with someone who never writes back.

Anyway, there I was, staring at ten rough-looking guys who were walking together swinging two-foot-long blades, cutting brush that had grown up along the side of the road.

"What am I doing here?" I asked God, which seemed to be a perfectly normal question. "Why would you send me on a wild goose chase for these men if they're cannibals or drug dealers?" I was shouting now. "If this is not what you want me to be doing, then please show me! Run me off the road. Flatten a tire. Topple a tree in front of this car. Because, God, if you don't stop me, I'm just going to keep on with this."

No sooner had I uttered the words when butterflies began to circle the car—hundreds, maybe thousands, of the loveliest, cream-colored creatures appeared, a kaleidoscope of butterflies flying around me as I barreled down the jungle road.

Whenever I share this part of the story, people try their best to explain it in non-spiritual terms: maybe it was the beginning of butterfly season in Mexico, or maybe the butterflies were attracted to the blue color of the car, or maybe I dreamed it. The funny thing is that I didn't initially see it as anything significant. I just thought it was weird to have all these butterflies with their almost transparent wings flying along with me. It didn't dawn on me until later that maybe God himself was enveloping me, affirming my journey, and ordering my path.

An hour and a half later, I saw the flashing yellow light in the distance and a sign pointing to San Blas. I slowed to make the turn, and soon I was driving through the middle of a village whose road was so bad I could barely clock ten miles per hour. Children who appeared to be younger than three years old—babies, really—were playing unsupervised near the road. Trash and debris were everywhere except in the town square where a Catholic church stood as if in protest to the squalor all around. This was the first of many villages I passed on the way to San Blas that fit this description, each in a similar state of disrepair and each town square and Catholic Church looking like the last one.

After forty-five minutes, I could see the ocean. It was breathtaking, a striking contrast to the jungle road that was lined with dilapidated houses, saloons, and unfinished condos. A late model black-and-white truck was approaching rapidly. As it got closer, I could see the light on top and realized it was a police vehicle. There were seven or eight men standing in the back armed with small machine guns. They passed me going about 70, and I could sense real danger. No one who cared for me, or could get me out of this country if I needed them to, knew where I was. The police obviously had bigger fish to fry. There were no mounted officers to preserve the peace. If something sinister were to happen to me, I might never be found.

An hour later, I at last reached San Blas, yet another town built around a square and a Catholic Church. I found my way to the Garza Canela, the hotel Josefina had described. I approached the front desk where a woman was working quietly. I asked if she was Josefina and reminded her that she was saving a room for me.

"We do have a room for tonight, but, as I said on the telephone, we are booked until Monday," she said curtly. "I can call the Flamingo and see if they have anything."

"That will be fine," I said. "Right now, I need you to help me."

"What do you mean?"

"I'm here to find the families of the three fishermen. I don't speak Spanish, and I need you to take me to where they live and translate for me."

She looked at me as if I had asked her to pull a rabbit out of a hat.

"No," she said emphatically.

"What? I can't do this on my own. If you don't help me, I'm dead in the water."

"I told you," she said, "there's a large group coming in tomorrow. I can't leave the hotel. Certainly you can understand."

"What am I supposed to do, Josefina?" I thought that if I said her name in the middle of my pleading, she might forget that we had just met and take me right to the fishermen.

"I am sorry," she said. Period. Game over.

I started to walk outside to get some air. A couple of years ago, this would have been the portion of the program where I smoked several cigarettes and had a tasty little mix of antidepressants and clear liquor. As I was walking toward the exit, a short Mexican man was standing just inside the door, blocking the way. He seemed to be expecting me.

"When do we start?" he said in English.

"Excuse me? You speak English?"

"Yes, of course, Bakersfield. Ten years. When do we start?"

"Are you saying you can help me?"

"Sure," he said casually.

"Right now?"

"Yes, right now." He spoke as if he had been waiting for me all day.

"Let me get a room and get cleaned up," I said. "I'll meet you in the bar in fifteen minutes."

He nodded, and I rushed through check-in and headed for my room. Looking at myself in the mirror, I saw that my beard was nearly a week old. I pulled a cheap hotel-issue razor from my bag. I had no shaving cream, so I spent the next few minutes lathering up a tiny bar of hand soap and proceeded to shave with a razor that was so dull it ripped the whiskers from my skin instead of cutting them. By the time I was done, I had half a dozen pieces of toilet paper on my neck. I looked like Freddy Krueger.

The guy who said he could help me was waiting in the hotel bar. He told me his name was Armando Santiago, and he knew he was holding all the cards. I leaned in close and started in.

"Armando," I said softly, "I'm here to see if I can find the fishermen, or the families of the fishermen. I've come to help them. I want to tell their story of faith, and I need you to translate and help me get around. I'll pay you. How much would you need?"

"I usually get $120 a day for taking people bird-watching," he said. Okay, so God in His infinite wisdom had decided to pair a Mexican bird-watcher with an American whose face was spotted with toilet paper to accomplish His purpose. Sure, why not? I agreed to Armando's rate, and he tapped his watch.

"We have to go before it gets dark, or we won't find anyone," he said impatiently.

"I know," I said. "But first I need you to understand what I'm trying to do so you can capture the emotion of what I'm saying when you translate."

I showed him an email exchange I had with Eli about how this seemed to be a story of hope and faith and asked him to look it over. He scanned the sheet of paper for all of forty-five seconds and looked up.

"Okay," he said. "I understand." When I asked him to tell me what he understood, he wasn't even close.

Armando suggested that our best bet was to try the city's director of tourism. It didn't make much sense to me that the first place we would go was the director of tourism's office, but Armando was all I had. I handed him the keys to the Fiesta, but he refused.

"I always let someone else drive," he said. "It's much safer that way." I wasn't sure if he meant "safer" from an insurance perspective or because drivers of blue rental cars often turned up drawn and quartered in back alleys.

19
Answers

I was driving toward the Pacific on a dirt road with potholes so deep that each time the Fiesta descended into one I held my breath as muddy water splattered the side windows. After a few blocks, Armando asked me to pull over in front of a rundown, salmon-colored building. We went inside just far enough to see a pair of steel-toed boots propped up on the arm of an old sofa. The boots belonged to a sleeping man who was wearing camouflage and cradling a rather large machine gun. Armando walked in like this was a common sight—a man taking an afternoon nap with an assault weapon—and the man began to stir. I backed out into the street, both to dissociate myself from Armando and to reduce the risk of my body being riddled with bullets. I decided to wait in the Fiesta.

Armando came out of the building.

"The tourism director is not here," he said. "We should try City Hall and look for the mayor."

He got back in the car, and we drove to the center of town, stopping across from the church in a busy square where many old men were hanging out. We walked through the main entrance of a half-painted building and into a large courtyard. Dozens of people were there, mostly talking on cell phones. They seemed out of place with their khakis, dress shirts, and shoulder bags. Of course, I was the only six-foot white guy within 100 miles. The air was buzzing, as if something big was about to happen. Armando excused himself; I stayed in the courtyard. To my left was a guy waiting on a bench with an expensive-looking camera hanging from his shoulder. There was a logo on his tan vest—TV Azteca. The press had arrived.

Armando peeked out and signaled for me to come into the office. I met the Mayor of San Blas, who couldn't speak any English. He was in the middle of arranging the fishermen's return to Mexico from the Marshall Islands. I also met Silverio, the city manager and apparently the number two man in San Blas, although I had a feeling he was really number one. After an exchange between Armando and Silverio in Spanish, and Armando and I in English, Silverio decided I was worthy to hear him directly in English. I arranged to meet with Silverio later that night. Apparently, he considered himself a dealmaker and someone who could speak for the fishermen. We left the mayor's office having learned nothing of value, and I paid Armando $120 for less than a day's worth of disappointment.

Back at the hotel, the news reports of the fishermen were rife with tales of cannibalism. I was discouraged but still held out hope—I had a meeting scheduled with Silverio. That night we were supposed to meet at the hotel at nine o'clock, but by eleven he hadn't shown. I went back to my room, flipped on the TV, and saw that the news coverage of the fishermen had hit a new low. As the news anchor read his copy, there was footage of the fishermen in Majuro to the left of his head and still photos of a plane crash to the right. They were comparing the fishermen's story to the Uruguayan rugby team whose airplane crashed in the Andes in 1972. The men who survived the crash were stranded for two months, and some of them fed on the dead bodies that were preserved in the snow. I shut the TV off and went to bed, counting my doubts instead of sheep.

This had been one of the longest days of my life.

At 4 a.m., I sat up in bed, wide awake. Instinctively, I grabbed my briefcase from the floor and began to rifle through it in the dark. During my many years on the road, I had often awakened at four in the morning in a hotel room and rifled through my briefcase for something to dull the pain. This time I was searching for my Bible, hoping to pray away my fear. I couldn't find it. I sat on the edge of the bed, with nothing else in the room with me but loneliness and anxiety. I dropped to my knees and asked God for direction.

"What do you want me to do?" I prayed in desperation. "Just show me and whatever it is, I'll do it!" Silence. I reached into my bag one more time, searching for an aspirin. This time, I brushed a corner of the Bible that had somehow gotten tucked into an unfamiliar pocket. I pulled it out, grabbed my glasses, and went into the bathroom. I flipped on the lights and sat down next to the sink. I had never played Bible Roulette, but it works like this: you open the Bible to whatever page your fingers find, hoping that the first verse you land on, especially in a moment of desperation, is *exactly what you need.* Sometimes it's something irrelevant involving the slaughter of goats, a plague, and lepers. But if you're lucky, the verse is life-changing, confetti drops from the heavens, and a brass band plays an up-tempo version of "Amazing Grace." As I sat alone in the fluorescent glow of the hotel bathroom, God gave me a simple message of grace that didn't require confetti or a brass band. The first words I saw: PRAY ABOUT EVERYTHING.

The verse was in Philippians, Chapter 4, and it got my attention. I read on. "Don't fret or worry. Instead of worrying, pray." *Maybe I should quit worrying about the rumors.* "Put into practice what you learned from me, what you heard and saw and realized. Do that, and God, who makes everything work together, will work you into his most excellent harmonies." *Work me into his most excellent harmonies?* I couldn't believe it. I asked God what to do, and 30 seconds later He gave me the only possible answer. Then it hit me—*Holy smokes! I am supposed to be here.* Everything else in my life had been a prelude to this moment: my personal experiences, professional experience, meeting Victoria, Eli not being able to go to San Blas, Josefina, the song on the radio, the first-class seat, the nudge to buy the ticket, the nun, the butterflies, Armando, and now this.

I knew that getting the fishermen's story was a long shot, but I also knew that something special was happening. I also thought no one would believe it. So I spent the next four hours recording every detail—from the day Victoria told me about the fishermen until the moment in the hotel at 4 a.m. I began to keep a diary of everything that occurred from that point on—every leg of the journey; every phone call, email, and prayer; notes about the weather and snippets of conversation; believing all of it mattered.

It was then I started to see all of this as more than a story for a book and perhaps a movie. When the sun came up, I could feel the momentum of something incredibly big. But I realized I couldn't just show up and say, *Hi, I'm Joe. Can I have your story?* I called my attorney and told her what I was doing. We agreed that if I ended up finding the fishermen and getting the story, it would be a good idea to have already formed a company. She said she could get it done in a day. She asked me what I wanted to call the company, and I remembered that night about a month earlier when I had written in my Bible that I was going to "stand in the gap."

"Ezekiel 22," I said. She said she would put things in motion, and we hung up. At breakfast the next morning, Armando and Silverio showed up with a guy named Eduardo, who seemed to be Silverio's right-hand man. I told them all the crazy coincidences that had happened since I arrived in Mexico—everything. Then I read them the Bible passage that answered my prayer. They just stared at me.

"Gentlemen," I said, "I think I am the one who is supposed to tell this story."

20

Reunions

I watched the press conference from my hotel room in Tepic; Eli watched it from Mexico City and translated everything via speakerphone. It was like watching a football game with the volume turned down on the television but listening to your favorite radio announcer give the play-by-play The Mexican TV networks were doing wall-to-wall coverage. What I didn't know was that the American networks were swept up in coverage of the extradition of JonBenet Ramsey's alleged killer.

Silverio and Eduardo had invited me to fly to Mexico City to meet the fishermen when they stepped off the plane from Los Angeles, but the Mayor of San Blas decided that he and the governor would go instead of the unknown gringo from out of town. Silverio asked me to meet him in Tepic, the state capital, because it was the airport where the fishermen were supposed to fly to after Mexico City. So I drove to Tepic that afternoon and met with Silverio, who laid out the fishermen's itinerary and gave me one of his cell phones so I could contact him easily. Unfortunately, it had no minutes left on it. While I was out buying more minutes, I bought a white linen suit thinking that when I finally met the men I should look professional and angelic. It seemed like a good idea at the time, but I never wore it.

When the three fishermen walked into the crowded press conference room at the Mexico City airport, they were all smiles, happy to be there. The flash of cameras lit up the room, and there was applause and cheering. It was as if they were the first Mexican astronauts to reach the moon. Then I saw their expressions change.

"What happened?" I shouted at the phone.

"They just asked them if they killed the other two guys and ate them," Eli said.

"What are the fishermen saying?" I yelled.

"One of them just said it's not true and that they have nothing to hide."

I felt sick. These guys didn't seem capable of anything so grand as a conspiracy. I was more determined than ever to find them and hear their story firsthand.

Silverio called and asked me to come to the Tepic airport. Before I did, I arranged for a lawyer to come from Mexico City to make sure that everything was on the up and up. I found Silverio in the thick of it, and he quickly introduced me to a governor's aide, some reporters, and Lucio's entire family—mother, father, brothers, sisters, uncles, aunts, and grandmother. Even the bishop was there. It was incredible.

"Where are Jesús' and Salvador's families?" I asked the aide. Then he dropped the bomb on me.

"Oh, they aren't from here," he said. "They're flying back to the cities they're from. I'm sorry no one told you."

Just then, a plane circled the Tepic airport and came in for a landing. Along with the crowd of family members, the bishop, and the governor's men, I was ushered onto the tarmac about 75 yards from where the plane stopped. It was surreal, and I looked incredibly out of place. There were only about two people out of 500 who spoke English. I was surrounded by Lucio's family, and none of them spoke English. Even worse, they didn't know who I was or what I was doing there. But we were one big happy family.

The cabin door opened and passengers started filing out. We watched a few dozen people who were not Lucio descend the stairs. Then, no one came out for a few moments. We waited in silence. Finally, the Mayor of San Blas stepped out of the plane, then the Governor, and, finally, Lucio. The band started playing, the crowd was cheering, and the family let out a collective gasp. Lucio slowly came down the four or five steps and started walking toward the crowd of relatives. When he got within twenty paces, his mother burst into tears and Lucio picked up his pace to a jog. The scene was electric. The family was silent, but everyone else was buzzing. It was controlled chaos until Lucio reached his mother, and then the flood gates opened.

I had never seen raw emotion like that before—I had just witnessed a man coming back from the dead. Then, seemingly out of nowhere, the media began to swarm around us. Dozens of reporters were pressing in on the family, and we became a giant moving mob, five persons deep, the news hounds pushing and elbowing to get to

Lucio. Silverio and I somehow managed to usher Lucio off the tarmac and into the governor's motor home. It was like a Michael Jackson sighting in the '80s.

I drove back to San Blas with the attorney and learned that he hadn't graduated from law school yet. In effect, he was just a $100-an-hour translator. He was a nice kid, though. When we got to the hotel, we found Silverio at the center of everything, overseeing Lucio's welcome-home celebration. There were about a thousand people in the courtyard of another San Blas hotel. Music was blasting, people were dancing and drinking. It was like *Cinco de Mayo* in August. We asked to see Lucio and were told he was resting. Silverio had not asked for money yet, which was encouraging even though I did offer to compensate him for all he had done. He and I agreed to meet the next day for lunch at Casa Manana. The meter on the kid was running, 24/7. He was going to be by my side for several days—$2,400 a day, plus expenses. I could hear a sucking noise coming from my 401k.

Silverio arrived the next day with the news that Lucio was at home and that the mayor had posted police officers with machine guns to keep the press out. I asked if I could get thirty minutes with Lucio to explain my vision for this story and let him know how important it was to make an official statement refuting the charges the press was making. I wanted Lucio to know that I was not one of those Hollywood guys who offers a small sum up front for the rights to the story then makes whatever movie he thinks will sell the most tickets. (A Hollywood studio executive later told me that the faith story was okay, but it wasn't the movie she would make. Her movie would be about the rumors—guns, murder, and conspiracy. The truth didn't seem to matter.)

Silverio told me he would try to get me an appointment with Lucio and would meet me for lunch the following day. When I arrived at the restaurant, Silverio was waiting with Eduardo. Apparently, they were now Lucio's "handlers." I found myself having to negotiate hard just to get five minutes with him. Finally, Eduardo said what I was afraid he would say.

"Well, you know," he said slowly, "there are other offers." These guys were playing me and I knew it. I decided to call their bluff.

"You know what, guys? I'm done. I'm on the next plane out of here. Thanks, but I've had enough." I slid my proposal across the table. "Here's my offer. You know how to find me." I told them that if they really had other offers, they should take one of them because the press was already calling the fishermen drug dealers, murderers, and cannibals. This story was going to be written with or without them, and the truth would run a poor second to whatever sold the most newspapers. Do me a favor, I said, and do the fishermen a favor, and take an offer. Then I walked away. I packed my bags and took the first flight out.

Carmen picked me up at the Atlanta airport, and I could tell she was nervous. She was trying to project enthusiasm and support, but I knew it was hard for her having to hold down the fort for so long. I had been gone for ten days, and we had had very little communication during that time. I sat quietly in the car as we left the terminal.

"So?" she said softly. It was a question she had every right to ask.

"I never got to meet the fishermen," I said without looking at her.

"How much money did you spend on this trip?" she asked without a hint of anger in her voice, which only made me feel worse.

"I don't know, and I don't want to know." We didn't speak for the rest of the trip home.

The next day at the office, I was greeted with the silent treatment. I tried to explain.

"This is a story of epic proportions that could inspire millions of people," I said, believing my own words even if no one else did. "I feel called to do this. I think God has big plans for...."

"It doesn't fit our model," said one of my partners, echoing what I had heard before I had left. *He was right about that, but what about all the things that had happened on this trip? Were they just a string of coincidences?*

It seemed like it was over. My wife thinks I've gone off the deep end. My partners want me out. I will now have no income again and I had already drained a big chunk of my 401k with the Summer of Joe. I was crushed.

Later that week, I got an email from Armando. He was with two of the fishermen, Jesús and Salvador. I called him right away and asked him what the men thought of my offer. He said they never heard of it. I told Armando that if he could get them to meet with me, I would be on the next plane to Mexico. He said he would get back to me.

I had planned to be in Colorado for a retreat, so I called my friend Reese, a pastor, to tell him I would have to skip the Colorado trip. He called back the next day.

"Joe," he said, "go back if you really think you need to, but if this is something God wants you to be part of, it will happen. If it's something He doesn't want you to be part of, it won't happen—and there isn't a thing you can do about it. If it's meant for you, it will be there when you get back from Colorado." I believed him. His advice was the beginning of a new understanding for me—trusting God with the outcome.

So I left my family for another week and flew to Colorado, which turned out to be the right move. I got to share all the stuff that had happened to me in Mexico, and I got a chance to be in God's country listening to Him every day among the majestic mountains He created. While I was there, Reese gave me another piece of good advice.

"If you are going to live in God's kingdom," he said, "it's going to take every ounce of passion and forcefulness you've got. Things are going to get fierce—that's why you were given a fierce heart." Then he looked me straight in the eye and said, "Do you have something better to do with your life?"

On the final day of the retreat, Reese gave us a photocopy of a prayer of protection and suggested we start every day with it.

Father,
Thank you for your angels. I summon them in the
authority of Jesus Christ and release them to war for me
and my household and my life and in my sphere of influ-

ence. *Thank you for those who pray for me. I know full well I need these prayers. I ask you to send forth your Spirit and raise these men and women up, arouse them, unite them, establish and direct them, raising up numerous prayers and intercessions for me. I call forth the Kingdom of the Lord Jesus Christ this day throughout my home, my family, my life, and all areas of my influence. All this I pray in the name of Jesus Christ, with all glory and honor and thanks to Him.*

That afternoon, I received word from Silverio that the fishermen were ready to meet with me on Tuesday morning at the Hotel Casa Manana. Tuesday was only a few days away, so I decided that instead of flying back to Atlanta, I would go directly to Mexico. I put together a PowerPoint presentation and prepared to at last meet with the three fishermen.

When the doors of the meeting room opened, my Mexican "team"—Silverio, Eduardo, Armando—and just one of the fishermen, Salvador, walked in with an entourage of friends, city officials, and the parish priest. I had flown in the kid attorney and Eli to translate. I asked Eli to ask them if they would give me a few minutes to explain why I was here, and if they didn't like what I had to say, I would never bother them again. Eli told them the entire story from the day Victoria told me about the fishermen right up to this moment—all the twists and turns and all the signs. Thirty minutes into the story, Padre Pedro, the 80-year-old priest, stood up and began to speak. Eli translated.

"He has just given his blessing," Eli told me. "He says he can see the kind of men we are, that we are men of God." After the padre's comments, Salvador said yes. One down, two to go.

Lucio wasn't at this meeting because no one could find him. He had been gone for about a week. I suggested we go to his house, about an hour away, and look for him. So Salvador, Eduardo, and couple of other guys piled into my car and headed to Lucio's grandmother's house, which is where he lived. He wasn't there. Then we went to his uncle's house. Lucio wasn't there, but his uncle, Remigio, was. Uncle Remigio was in his mid-forties, with speckled grey hair and a voice that sounds like he's singing when he talks. The first time I met him, he greeted me with a handshake, wearing just pants. No shirt. No shoes. Just pants. We are roughly the same age, but he looks sixty. His hands and feet were rough and worn like seasoned catcher's mitts. I went through my PowerPoint presentation for a man with no shirt on and several other people who I suspect were relatives of Lucio. I doubt that any of them understood any of it. Afterward, I closed my computer and asked my audience, with the help of Eduardo, "Where is Lucio?"

His uncle was the only one to answer, shrugging his shoulders. He had no idea. Just then, Lucio came strolling up the path. I did a shortened version of the presentation again and asked Lucio what he thought of it. Salvador said something in Spanish to Lucio. Lucio said something in Spanish to his uncle, who nodded. Lucio looked at me, smiled, and gave me the "okay" sign and a nod. That was all I needed. I had Salvador and Lucio. Now all I had to do was find Jesús.

21

Muscles And Miracles

Fortunately, someone had a piece of paper that had a number for Jesús. Lucio's aunt went into their hut and came back with a telephone in her hand, unwound the wire, and plugged it into a jack outside. She dialed the number and handed the phone to Salvador, who repeated everything he was hearing from the other end of the line to Eduardo. After a brief exchange with Eduardo, I found out that Jesús didn't want to be bothered. The governor of his state was coming to see him next week. *Next week?* I was losing my mind. I needed 30 minutes with the guy. I couldn't imagine he was tied up between now and the meeting with the governor unless he had hired a publicist, booked Oprah, Dave, and Jay, with a little Regis and Kelly on the side. I had to use a little muscle. I told Eduardo to tell Salvador to tell Jesús that I couldn't wait—that I would go wherever he was, but it had to be by tomorrow. Jesús finally agreed to meet me at ten the next morning in front of the Cathedral in Mazatlan, about six hours north.

I decided to risk driving there at night because I didn't want to take a chance on missing Jesús. It was about 5 p.m., and I figured we could be on the road by 6 p.m. Eduardo translated my orders to the others. They looked as if I had said, "This is a suicide mission, men, but we're going to do it anyway." Eduardo said they were not going to drive there at this hour. Too dangerous.

"Well, I'm going tonight," I said confidently.

I asked Eduardo to have Lucio and Salvador there early so we could meet as a group. Eduardo drove a 1972 blue Chevy van that had rusted-out honeycomb rims, a badly airbrushed exterior, blue velvet interior, and no air-conditioning. I fondly referred to it as the Scooby-Doo Mystery Machine.

I found myself driving through the Mexican jungle again, this time at night, again without a map. The only directions I was given were to "follow the road to Tepic until it ends, then turn left for the next five hours." Amazingly, I made it with no major issues. Apart from a handful of people in San Blas, no one knew where I was. If I somehow ended up in one of these ravines in the jungle, no one would ever find me. It was about 1 a.m. when I arrived, and I was exhausted. I pulled up to a taxi stand and asked where I could find the best hotel in town. Several of the drivers pointed to the building where their cabs were parked. I was so tired, I had to trust them. I got a room at the Pueblo Bonita and slept better than I had in weeks.

The next morning I awoke around seven, put on a T-shirt, a pair of shorts, and flip flops, grabbed my Bible, the prayer I had gotten earlier in the week, and headed downstairs, past the pool to the café to get a cup of coffee. Then I walked down to the beach. The hotel actually was very nice, and the employees were buzzing around the property in their khaki shorts, flower-print shirts, and sneakers, cleaning everything in sight. I sometimes joke that people in Mexico clean the dirt—but it's true. I can't tell you how many times I've watched a woman hunched over a dirt path, sweeping and getting the dirt as clean as she can. I enjoyed watching them work as I sipped my coffee. Throughout this entire crazy adventure, everyone I had met in Mexico had been kind to me, and in that moment I was very grateful. I stepped down to the beach, grabbed a chair, and sank down into it. I had tucked the prayer from my Colorado trip in my Bible, and I read it aloud.

When I finished, I bowed my head again, feeling the need for something more. This was it. The Big Day—the first time I would have all three of the fishermen together in one place. The stakes were high, and doubt quickly began to creep in. I had been shown some amazing signs over the last few weeks that I knew were meant to show me that I was on the right path. But, today I needed one more nod of approval so I could truly believe. So, I asked Him: "Okay, God, you've shown me a lot this week, and it seems that this is where you've been leading me. If this is *really* what you want me to do, then I'll commit to it with everything I have. But I need you to show me one more sign."

I was hoping for something along the lines of a flaming cross on the mountaintop or a lightning bolt coming out of a clear blue sky, you know, an Old Testament-style confirmation that I wasn't insane. I would have settled for giant letters in the sand spelling out the Nike slogan.

But there was no flaming cross, no lightning bolt, no letters in the sand. I sat there feeling a bit silly. Maybe I had asked for one sign too many. Perhaps God was just sitting on His throne in heaven rolling His eyes. Maybe He had had it with me. Maybe He was throwing up his hands and saying, "Enough already!"

What an idiot. And that's me I'm talking about, not God. I was asking the Alpha and the Omega for magic on my terms. I started laughing at the absurdity of it. I had come so far and had so many nods from God that this was right, and yet I was demanding one more confirmation from Him that this is what He wanted.

Feeling foolish and alone, I walked up the stairs from the beach and turned right to go to my room to prepare for my meeting with the fishermen. Then I felt it, another nudge. It was like a voice, but not an audible one, telling me, "Go back over there, and ask that guy his name." On the deck, twenty yards in the opposite direction, I saw a guy with his back to me setting up umbrellas by the pool. I did an about-face and walked toward him. When I got within three feet, I stopped. He had no idea I was behind him. Then I did it.

"*Como se llama?*" I asked. Even before he started to turn around, I knew what was about to happen. First, I knew that God was laughing at me for trying to get Him to do things my way, and, second, I had a sensation I can only describe as electric and otherworldly. I knew what was going to be on his nametag. In my mind's eye, I could see it as clear as if I were already looking at it. I knew what his name was before he turned around—Jesús.

I heard him say the word the same moment his nametag came into view. This was it. The sign I had prayed for. I was just starting to learn that God rarely does things the way I expect. He does things His way, sometimes in grand, sweeping gestures and others in subtle whispers. Jesús was the only fisherman I had yet to meet, and I had been apprehensive about moving forward. I needed a sign and God delivered. I have no doubt that it was His nudge on the stairs that directed me back to the man by the pool.

I looked up to the sky and said in a voice no one but God could hear, "I'm in. I'm all in. I will do whatever it takes. I get it, God. You don't have to show me anything else."

Meanwhile, the young man stood there staring at me, smiling expectantly. He was waiting for the follow-up question, but God hadn't given me one. After a few seconds of awkwardness, I thanked him and walked away. *No one will ever believe this*, I thought to myself. Then I had an idea. I rushed back to Jesús, the sign from God, and asked him in broken Spanish to sign his name on the copy of the prayer I had read on the beach. It took a few tries, but he finally understood what I was asking when I mimed the international pen-to-paper motion. I was elated. I must have said, "*Gracias*" five times. What happened next is a blur.

I drove downtown for my meeting with the three fishermen and parked a few blocks off the main square. I took a seat on a bench across from the cathedral, giddy with expectation. It was about 9:15 a.m., and Jesús, the third fisherman, was due to arrive at 10. I spent the next hour teetering between hope and disappointment. I would later learn that Jesús was never on time, a piece of information that would have been helpful to have. I was going out of my mind.

Eleven-thirty and still no sign of Jesús. I began to worry that maybe I had missed him, that maybe he had already come and gone. I walked around the square, peeking in a few of the shops. A dozen scenarios went through my mind, like what if Jesús was the lone holdout and I would only be able to sign *"Dos Pescadores?"* If that happened, I might as well have zero *pescadores*. I chewed on that unsavory morsel for a while and then moved on to Eduardo: Why wasn't he here? What if he's led Salvador and Lucio to another offer? I worked over every possibility in my head and went back to my bench.

At 12:15, two guys crossed the street and headed toward me. It was Jesús! I jumped off the bench, so relieved that I stuttered his name as they walked past me. Jesús turned around and smiled.

"Hola, Jesús, mi amigo," I said. *"Me llamo Joe."* He looked surprised that I was speaking Spanish. I was surprised that I was speaking Spanish. I approached him with an outstretched arm, and he reached out and shook my hand eagerly and launched into a rapid-fire dialogue with me that was entirely one-sided because, let's face it, I had no idea what he was saying. I guess since I had opened in Spanish, he thought I could speak the language. I tried to follow along, feebly, and I think he may have introduced his little friend, whose name I didn't

catch. I was sure, though, that Jesús was a good guy. He seemed sincere, which was comforting.

I asked Jesús if he was hungry, nodding in the direction of the pizza place. I'm not sure if they understood, so I started walking toward the restaurant and they followed. I kept my eyes peeled for Eduardo and the rest of the gang, but there was no sign of them. This was the first of many times I would want to smack Eduardo. But, he was my translator, and I needed him.

I motioned for Jesús and his friend to order while I fired up my laptop and dove into my presentation. Despite my limited Spanish, I thought I was doing a good job because Jesús seemed interested and nodded occasionally. I later learned that nodding occasionally could also indicate that a person has no idea what you're talking about. When I got to the part about money, though, Jesús carefully pored over the numbers. I half-expected him to pull out a green eyeshade. Apparently, he was fluent in the universal language of "How much is this worth to me?" He looked up from the paper with the numbers and said, "*Mas.*" For those of you who don't possess my advanced language skills, that means "More." The fisherman with the grade-school education was already negotiating for more.

"Maybe," I said, hedging my bet. "It could be more; it could be less." He looked at the numbers again and mumbled something like, "Is this amount just for me?"

"No," I said. "This is for *tres pescadores*—not *uno pescador.*" He shook his head violently, which I took to mean that this was not acceptable.

The pizza arrived just in time. I excused myself and went to look for Eduardo. I found him and the others wandering around the square, sweating like they had just gotten out of a sauna—or the Scooby-Doo van. I ushered them inside and motioned for them to order. They weren't interested in eating; they just wanted to talk to Jesús.

This would be the second time I wanted to smack Eduardo. I had spent weeks trying to get these guys together in the same room, and Eduardo all of a sudden decides that he holds all the cards. He ripped into Jesús in Spanish, ignoring my requests for a translation. All I could do was watch as Jesús became angry, raising his voice and saying no to something that, of course, I couldn't understand because Eduardo was not translating. In fact, Eduardo was brushing me off as if I were a nuisance. *The American guy over there? Yes, he is annoying, isn't he?* I was ready to tear my hair out.

Salvador and Lucio seemed bewildered for a few moments. Then everyone at the table was yelling at each other, right there in the Mexican pizza place, while I sat there with my mouth hanging open, watching everything crumble before my eyes.

"What is going on here?" I said in my best I-mean-business voice.

"Jesús wants to have a lawyer look at the contracts," Eduardo shot back, "and I told him that he has to sign now."

"You're not a lawyer," I said, exasperated, "and you're not my negotiator. The only thing you should be doing right now is translating. Nothing more."

"I know how to handle these guys," he insisted.

"He doesn't have to sign *anything* right now," I said firmly. "Of course he can have a lawyer look at this." I dialed Eli in Mexico City, in part because I knew he would be able to sort this out, but mostly because I needed something to do with my hands other than smack Eduardo.

"Eli, I need your help here. Jesús is about to punch Eduardo and so am I. He's telling Jesús he has to sign this document right now. Please talk to him." I tried to hand the phone to Jesús but he refused.

"Eli, he won't take the phone."

"Joe, he won't talk to me because he doesn't know me. Let me talk to one of the others."

I wasn't about to give the phone to Eduardo, so I gave the phone to David, who was a friend of Salvador. David and Eli had a brief conversation, then David talked with the other men at the table. Suddenly, everyone was nodding amiably. David handed the phone back to me.

"What just happened, Eli?"

"They've agreed to let us tell their story, pending having a lawyer look over the document. They will sign a letter of intent today."

I hung up the phone and we all shook hands. I invited everyone for lunch. I wanted to take them someplace quiet, perhaps someplace with a tablecloth and linen napkins. I asked Eduardo if he knew of such a place where we could continue to talk and share a meal while my lawyers back home drafted the letter of intent. Eduardo said he was very familiar with Mazatlan and knew of a place in the Sands Hotel that would be perfect—on the beach. Señor Frog's.

We piled into two cars: my rental and the afore-mentioned Scooby-Doo van. I found the Sands Hotel but quickly discovered that Señor Frog's had moved to a building farther down the beach. When I got there, the rest of the gang was waiting outside. For some reason, I had trusted Eduardo to select the dining establishment. Note to self: Never let a guy driving a Scooby-Doo van pick the restaurant. When we walked in at 1:30 in the afternoon, there was a woman dancing on a table and the music was so loud you couldn't hear the person next to you if he were screaming at the top of his lungs.

"This is the place you pick for us to sit down and talk?" I shouted to Eduardo. "You actually think this is appropriate?" He shrugged. We all got back in our cars and drove to a restaurant at the Saba Hotel that was cool, quiet, with no "Jungle Party Yard of Beer" on the menu. Everyone ordered, and I stepped outside to call the law firm and check on the paperwork. They emailed the documents to me, and I printed copies for everyone to sign.

After the three fishermen signed the letter of intent and the shock wore off, it started to sink in that I had gotten the story. *Really kind of miraculous*, I thought for just a moment. There was no time for me to celebrate or dwell on how emotionally exhausted I was from the frenzied weeks of searching and coming up empty-handed, the days I had wasted spinning my wheels waiting for people who never showed up, spending money I didn't have, the moments I felt the hand of God on me and the moments I felt completely alone and scared, drowning my sorrows in chips and salsa. I had to shelve any feelings of triumph or tragedy. There was simply no time for any of that. It was time to crank my rusty Hollywood publicity machine.

22

My Plan

The strategy was simple: put out the word and wait for the offers to come pouring in. I got in touch with a friend at *Variety* who already had read some information that had been leaked to the media, namely an article in which Silverio, speaking out of turn, told the media that I had paid as much as $4 million for the rights to the fishermen's story, which wasn't true, but once something like that gets into print, even in an obscure Mexican newspaper, you might as well forget about trying to set the record straight. When I told this to my friend at *Variety*, he instantly launched into a bigger-than-a-breadbasket-smaller-than-a-school-bus thing—"Less than $4 million but bigger than $3 million?" Geez.

Eventually, I was able to divert the money questions and get the release out. It wasn't long before the phone started ringing. First, the Mexican press, who were more interested in the rumors of cannibalism than the truth. As the coverage gained speed, what unfolded was a classic Salem Witch Trial of misinformation. The media were simply reporting what other people in the media said. No one seemed to be doing the legwork required to get the facts. The U.S. media were busy covering the JonBenet story. It was a mess, but I kept on hoping that the truth would eventually surface.

Meanwhile, I spent time interviewing the fishermen as a group, then individually, and their stories were similar, though not identical. At first these seeming inconsistencies concerned me, but then a friend reminded me that each of the men saw what happened through a different lens. Besides, if the details matched perfectly, the story was probably rehearsed.

Soon I was getting calls from major magazines—*Men's Journal, GQ,* the *New Yorker, The Sunday London Times.* Each of them had assigned a reporter to write their own version of the story. It was clear during the interviews which writers had made up their minds what the story was before they met the fishermen or me. I understood that the cannibalism and drug-trafficking angles were appealing. Who wants to write a good old-fashioned survival tale when there might be blood, guts, and guns involved? Most of the interviews I did left me feeling like I had been stabbed in the back. I suppose I took it so personally because I had spent so much time with the fishermen and thought I could appreciate how different their lives were from mine. All three of them had been born into extreme poverty. Food, health care, education—none of these were a given. Before these guys ever set foot on that *panga,* they were already in a survival situation. I get freaked out just because the Wi-Fi at Starbucks isn't working. Jesús, Salvador, and Lucio simply swapped one set of difficult circumstances on land for another set on the sea and made the best of it.

After the initial wave of media interest, I laid low and started to outline what I hoped would be something—a book or a movie—that would allow me to set the record straight. Some friends who knew the story invited me to speak at their church one Sunday about the fishermen and their faith, and I accepted. When I finished my presentation, a woman approached me to say I was telling the story wrong. I thought this was a bit strange and more than a little bold, but I listened. She said my own journey of faith was an essential part of the story. I agreed to meet with her again, mostly because she was getting her Ph.D. in Rhetoric and was certain to know more about story structure than I did.

We met a few times a week over the next month or so. She was unrelenting in her belief that combining the two story lines—the fishermen's and mine—was the best approach, but I remained unconvinced. I wasn't even sure exactly what my story was, other than a man who went a little bit crazy, found God, then spent a rumored $4 million on a survival tale involving turtle blood and hints of cannibalism. I didn't get that my journey might be of interest to anyone other than my therapist and me. She kept pressing, and I kept dodging, and we worked that way for several weeks. We actually made some progress toward something I needed: getting this all down on paper to prove this story was real, that it actually happened—and that I was there.

I flew out to Los Angeles with my story rights and some ideas of what I wanted the story of *Tres Pescadores* to look like. For some reason, telling the story visually seemed much easier to me. I really didn't know where to start, so I started with what I knew—TV. I set up a series of meetings with some old friends from my TV days, hoping the smallness of Hollywood would allow me to step seamlessly into the movie neighborhood. Oddly enough, this included the guy whose job I had said I wanted all those years ago during my red carpet days. He was now CEO at one of the smaller studios. He had had one of his development people talk with me about the project a few weeks earlier. I met her at their offices in Santa Monica, and she took me down to the commissary to chat. I told her the story. Two other executives, the heads of this and that, joined us, and she introduced me to everyone and asked me to tell the story of the fishermen, which I did. When I was done, they all exchanged glances.

"Now, tell them the other story," she said.

"What other story?" I didn't get it at first.

"The one about you." There was an awkward pause, and then I launched into it. About two minutes in, they all exchanged glances again in their all-powerful, all-knowing Hollywood way. I waited.

"That's Act Two," said one of them.

"What does that mean?" I asked him.

"It means this story needs a character like you," he said. "Three Mexican men on a boat speaking Spanish isn't a feature film; it's a documentary that nobody in the U.S. will want to see. But if we put a guy like you in the story, then guys like you will go see it."

"This is not about me," I said. "This is their story— their survival, their rescue, their faith. I can't be part of this."

"If you want anyone to see this movie," he said, "you'll have to get over that."

I left the meeting confused. At least I knew there was interest in the story, but it bothered me that these guys thought three men surviving nine months at sea was not marketable unless my wacky life was tacked onto it.

In January, a friend of mine called to give me the name of a reporter at the *Atlanta Journal-Constitution* who he thought should hear the story. The reporter interviewed Carmen and me and sent a photographer who took some shots of me wearing a warm-up jacket and holding a Bible, sort of an Old Testament track star. I didn't plan to represent Team Jesus this way; it's just what I happened to have on. Also, my hair was a little long and mangy, completing my Old Testament look and no doubt causing many a suburban housewife to wonder how Carmen could have allowed me to appear before nearly one million readers without considering what was going on on top of my head.

The story was set to appear a week later on the front page of the Sunday edition. It must have been a slow news week. The Saturday night before the story ran, I picked up my daughter and her friends from a swim meet then stopped at a convenience store to see if they had the early edition of the Sunday paper. There it was: a six-by-six-inch photo of me on the front page under the headline "A Test of Faith." All I can say is that it's bizarre to see yourself on the cover of anything. I picked up two more papers and resisted the urge to tell the cashier that you-know-who was on the cover.

Back in the car, I took a deep breath and handed a paper to each of them. "This is crazy, Dad," my 12-year-old daughter said in a way that I knew she was partly excited but mostly embarrassed. "It takes up the whole page."

To my daughters this was unwanted notoriety. An image of their dad posing as an athletic but slightly unkempt religious zealot on the front page of the Sunday paper was going to be strange for them when they walked into school Monday morning. I don't know how it went for them at school, but the article did fuel further interest in the story.

I was invited to the Sundance Film Festival, and there were several offers to do a film. I didn't know much about the movie business, but I did know enough to say no to a bad offer. I turned them down because I felt I had an obligation to the fishermen to tell the story the way it deserved to be told and for them to be compensated fairly. Eventually, however, I accepted the idea of a "fourth fisherman," who would be a character modeled after me, and, after exhausting every possible excuse, I started to write my story.

23
The Plan

A month before a flurry of articles in the U.S. and Europe about the fishermen and my role in the story appeared in *The New Yorker, Mens Journal, GQ, Der Spiegel,* and other major publications, Carmen and I were sitting in a counseling session together. The counselor had heard both of us talk about this project and how we felt about it. I still wanted to go all out; Carmen was supportive but wary.

"Can you be his cheerleader for one year?" the counselor asked Carmen, who looked at me for a few moments before answering.

"Yes, I suppose I can," she said. I immediately felt a tremendous sense of relief. We were on the same team, and I was more confident than ever. Interesting how two people can interpret the same simple sentence so differently. What I heard was, "We're going all the way with this." What Carmen heard, however, was, "If nothing concrete happens by December 31, 2007, at 11:59 p.m., then Joe agrees to drop this project."

I spent most of that summer writing a screenplay and a rough draft of a book. Meanwhile, our savings shrank and the tension grew, although I was often oblivious to both. The year went by and nothing concrete happened— that is, nothing we could take to the bank.

January 1, 2008, came and went, and I was still as confident as ever that what I was doing was God-ordained and would ultimately pan out. Carmen felt betrayed. It didn't help that I told her I needed to go to the Sundance Film Festival again. I don't think she doubted I was trying to do what I felt was God's will, but I know she sometimes wondered why God wasn't moving faster, if this was what He really wanted. She would occasionally say a prayer something on the order of, "Lord, please make something happen or make it end."

On many occasions, it did appear that I was on the verge of making something happen with the movie. *This is it*, we both thought each time. But it didn't happen. I did meet an up-and-coming Greek director who loved the story of the fishermen and wanted to be part of it. And of all the directors I could have run across, he turned out to be an award-winning, half-Latino-half-Greek who recently became a Christian. I took this as another sign that I should stay the course.

Around that time, I was meeting with a friend, and I was wondering if I was really being led by God to keep going. She said, "God can just as easily say yes to you or no to you now as He did when you were in Mexico." Fifteen seconds later, I received this unsolicited email:

Standing in the Gap

TGIF Today God Is First Volume 1 by Os Hillman
Friday, January 18, 2008
*I looked for a man among them who would build up
the wall and stand before Me in the gap on behalf of
the land so I would not have to destroy it, but I found
none.*—Ezekiel 22:30

I had named my company Ezekiel 22 a year and a half
ago because I had decided to stand in the gap. I said to
my friend who was sitting there as shocked as I was, "I
guess we'll keep going."

Every time I would come to the end of my rope—or
I thought I had pushed Carmen to the end of hers—God
would show me something, a small sign of encouragement, nothing more than the tiniest glimmer of hope,
and I would eat it up. It would be enough to feed me, and
often Carmen, for a little while longer, like manna from
the sky.

A cynic might say I was desperate, grasping at straws
to justify the time, energy, and money I had invested in
this project. A cynic might say I should have folded my
cards rather than stay in a high-stakes game and try to
draw to an inside straight. A cynic might be able to make
a pretty good case that I was just an egocentric fool who
went on a wild goose chase and didn't have the guts to
admit it.

I can't deny that there were moments I felt that way
myself.

We sold the lake house in February, which eased Carmen's mind a bit about our financial situation, even
though she admitted she had loved it when we were there

together as a family. To my way of thinking, selling the lake house bought me more time. Over the next year, I spent an inordinate amount of that time with my Greek director, leaving just about everything else in our life to be taken care of by Carmen. I know she was angry during this period and thought I was being self-indulgent, but she somehow managed to send me an encouraging email periodically.

Almost a full year after Carmen's cheerleading stint had expired, we had this exchange over transferring funds from one account to another so she could pay some bills, which was another unpleasant reminder that our finances were dwindling:

Dear Carmen,

Thank you, Honey, for doing this. Pray for a miracle.

Love
Your loser husband

She wrote back:

Joe,

Praying is our best option. Let's hope that the cash truck turns down our street sooner rather than later. We have got to really tighten our belts.

By the way, you are not a loser. You have had a dream that you have followed for the last two years...that is not something a loser does. You have given it your all...that is not something a loser does. Keep the faith. Even if it does not come out in the end the way you planned it, haven't

*you enjoyed the journey? You are smart, cute, and funny.
2009 will be full of new horizons. I just know it will be
good!*

Love you,
Carmen

I clung tightly to those emails like a frightened cat
stranded atop a telephone pole, even though I knew that
fear walked alongside Carmen most of the time. Over the
course of our marriage, she had prayed that God would
give her a godly man for a husband, and I think this is
what sustained her during the toughest trials. She could
see that I was genuinely seeking God with my whole heart,
which is what Jesus said it would take to find Him. Still,
we could both feel the distance between us. God was
testing Carmen's faith even as I was trying her patience.

In early 2009, I once again felt we were getting closer
on the movie. A Hollywood talent agent said he was certain
he could get a big-name star interested. All our troubles
would be over, or so we thought. The deal fell through
with a resounding thud. I had hit a wall. Each glimmer
of hope for a movie deal was being dashed. Was this the
end? Why would God take me this far only to let me
fall flat on my face? I struggled with this question for
months, and I was glad I had a group of guys around me
who I could talk with about all of this.

We had to sell Carmen's car in the spring to cover
some expenses, and I felt awful about it. Funny thing is,
she had never wanted an expensive car in the first place.
She would have been happy with a used Honda. I guess I
had bought it for her to make myself feel successful. Her

only regret was that now she would have to share one car with two teenagers.

In mid-July, we were broke. I had given a half-hearted effort to find a job, and Carmen had just about had it. I was as discouraged as I had ever been. We had garage sales, sold furniture, clothes, anything we didn't absolutely have to keep. I cashed in some of my life insurance policies. The IRS was contacting us about taxes and penalties due as a result of my draining the 401k. The credit card companies started sending letters and calling, and the company that financed our car was threatening to repossess it.

I poured out my soul in an email to a friend. "Until you and Carmen are in alignment," he wrote back, "I doubt this will ever go anywhere. Unless you bring her into the journey with you, she will never be willing or able to accept the consequences that go with sacrifice and walking by faith."

Is that what this is all about? My marriage? Is it possible that God...?

That was it. In my mind, Carmen and I had been in this together all along. But the reality was that I had been the one out there flying fast and free—the kite—and she had been left holding the string.

We had been out of counseling for more than a year, but I had an outlet. Four other men and I had decided to form a group that would be a lifelong open-ended commitment to be in each other's lives. One day we were meeting, and one of them asked me if Carmen and I were seeing a counselor. I told him we weren't, mostly because of the expense. They came to me later and offered to pay for our counseling, so there was no excuse for us not to go. These are incredible guys. True friends. I told Carmen I wanted to go back into counseling with her. I wanted us to be on the same team again.

A few months later, out of the blue, I got a call from a friend who wanted to introduce me to an editor he had worked with. I met with the guy and told him about the movie project and about the book I wanted to do after the movie came out. My plan was to do the movie first. The movie was going to be the cinematic version of the story of the fishermen. The book was going to be the story behind the story of the fishermen, and how these two separate stories have come together to form something larger than we could have imagined. He read some of what I had written and suggested we move forward with the book now. As we went over the rough manuscript, he kept asking at different points, "How did your wife feel about that?" Or "What did she say when you told her that?" He said I couldn't write a book about how chasing the fishermen story affected my faith walk without saying how it affected my wife and my marriage.

I told him I wasn't sure that Carmen would want to be in the book. She is a very private person, I said. He offered to talk with her about it and see if he could ease any concerns she might have. As I drove home that night, I thought about what my friend had written to me in July, his insight that I needed to bring Carmen into the journey with me. It was almost identical to what my editor was saying.

When I brought it up with Carmen, her reaction was predictable. "Joe, this is your story. I don't see why I need to be in it." I didn't push it. A few days later, I brought it up again. In the meantime, she had read the book my editor had written about a crisis in his marriage and how God had restored it. His wife shared her point of view in the story. This time, Carmen agreed to meet with him.

About a month earlier, I had started to read the so-called wisdom books of the Bible—Job, Psalms, Proverbs, Ecclesiastes, Song of Songs. I had never focused on a set of books or themes from the Bible before, but I found myself especially drawn to Ecclesiastes and Proverbs as I tried to sort out why my life had become so chaotic. These books are all about Folly and Wisdom. I decided to look at Folly first because I've had more of that in my life. I looked at it through the lens of Pass/Fail:

Start With God—FAIL.

Make Insight Your Priority—FAIL.

Don't Assume You Know It All—FAIL

Never Take Love For Granted—FAIL

One Who Knows Much Says Little—FAIL

Under the heading of Wisdom, I could only think of one thing: A Wife Of Noble Character—PASS. It was the only one I got right.

In our next counseling session, I admitted how foolish I had been with so many things. Carmen looked at me as if I were speaking Portuguese. But I could see the tenderness in her eyes as I talked about our marriage, our money, my health, and the folly of my life. I could feel her pain piercing my heart. I don't think she had seen this coming. Several seconds passed. Maybe she was thinking this was some sort of trick.

"Now I feel bad because you feel bad," she said finally.

"It's a good kind of feeling bad," I said.

The next morning, a friend called me in response to an email I sent him asking for his advice. I was out of money, the movie seemed stalled, and I needed income. He invited me to his office on Saturday. Carmen was excited, thinking that the meeting might lead to a job.

"You need to put this whole Christian thing behind you," he said just seconds after I sat down. "That's what you do on Sunday. You need to get back to the real world and forget all that stuff." He told me that many of my friends and former colleagues were worried about me. They felt that this whole "Christian thing" was just a phase I was going through. I understood. There was a time I would have thought I was a crackpot Jesus freak, too. He was just trying to rescue me from the madness.

"Finish the book," he said, "then put it all behind you."

When I got home, Carmen asked how it went. I told her.

"That must have really hurt you," she said gently.

"He was only trying to help."

Angel on one shoulder: "Stay the course. Be patient. Your heart is right. God has things under control."

Devil on the other shoulder: "Are you nuts? You could be making $200-$300K in no time. Welcome back, Porsche 911."

The next day, we were on our way to church in a driving rainstorm to hear the second part of a sermon series about taking responsibility for your life. Our pastor, Andy, spoke of a phrase he used to hear his father say when he was a kid: "Later and Greater." The message was simple: What we sow today we reap later, and what we reap is always much greater than we expect it to be, which can be really good or really bad. I thought about the seeds

I've sown. Some of the great seeds are my two wonderful daughters. Carmen gets most of the credit for them.

"Honey, I've sown some lousy seeds in my life, especially in our marriage," I said as soon as we got in the car. "We've been reaping—you've been reaping—things you don't deserve." The only sound was the rain pounding the roof of the car.

"I hope you can forgive me someday," I said. "I wouldn't blame you if you didn't." She remained silent as we drove to the grocery store. We parked near the front entrance, and Carmen continued to stare straight ahead.

I looked at her. "Can I ask you a question?" She nodded. "Have you ever considered that what I've done with the fishermen, I've done for you—for us?"

She didn't move.

"Have you ever considered that I do what I do so the kids will see their father as a man who is willing to take risks on things he says he believes in?"

Silence.

"Have you considered that I do what I do to glorify God, to be a blessing to others?" I was speaking almost in a whisper now. "Have you considered that the seeds I've sown with this fishermen story might one day reap something greater than either of us could have imagined?"

She continued to stare straight ahead.

"Is it possible that this is what we have had to go through to heal our marriage?" I went on. "That we've had to be stripped of everything so that there's only us and God. No cushions. No insulation. No medicines, including the anesthetic of money to keep us from feeling the pain?"

A tear ran down her cheek. Then another. Then a flood.

"I'm just tired," she said, sobbing. "I want it to be over. Why am I always the bad guy?" I leaned over and put my hand on hers.

"You're not the bad guy," I said. "You're not to blame for any of this." She turned to look at me.

"Even if you decided you want out of this marriage, I wouldn't blame you," I said, squeezing her hand. "No matter what you do, I will always love you."

She smiled. "Go get the groceries," she said.

24
His Plan

The next day was clear and bright, and I sensed something new in the air. Carmen had agreed to talk to my editor about her perspective on things. Three years after I had said, "Honey, I think I have to go to Mexico," she was ready to be part of telling this story. She was nervous. I dropped her at my offices, introduced her to my editor, and went to another meeting about the movie. When I picked her up ninety minutes later, she was in a playful mood.

"How was it?" I asked.

"It was good," she said.

I didn't press her for details. She gave me her to-do list for the day, and we ran errands together for the rest of the afternoon. She laughed. I laughed.

"I like this," I said after about an hour of driving her around.

"Maybe you should get a job as a chauffeur," she said.

"No. I mean I like hanging out with you, doing nothing, together. I could see us doing this on a regular basis."

"Me, too," she said. "Me, too."

That evening we had a session with our counselor. "So, how are you guys doing?" he asked. There was the usual awkward silent moment where we look at each other knowing that whoever speaks first is the one in the cross-hairs.

"Great!" I said.

"Tell me what that means," he said. I told him about the weekend and the conversation that started in the church parking lot and ended at the grocery store, how I admitted I had been foolish and how Carmen had cried, about the freshness of the next day and the sense of renewal, about the feeling of joy and connectedness I had while I was playing chauffeur. Carmen agreed.

"Congratulations!" he said. "Sixteen sessions and you've finally de-escalated the negative dynamic of the dance of your power struggle."

Carmen and I looked at each other and smiled. We just thought we were having a good day.

A week later, I apologized to Carmen for all the times I was insensitive and self-absorbed. I looked over at her and thought to myself, *How did I ever get so far away from being the man she deserved to have in her life? Why did I think that some sort of accomplishment, even in the name of God, could be a substitute for the nourishment, energy, and love that my wife needed?*

"It's so nice to finally hear you acknowledge how painful this has been for me," she said. "It makes me want to forgive...." She collected herself and started again. "It allows me to forgive you."

I could feel the weight lifting from her shoulders.

* * *

I've learned a lot of things over the past few years. One is that God can take you to some strange and scary places if you let Him—and I'm not just talking about geography. Another is that I didn't need to go to another country or make a big score to find unconditional love. God already loved me that way, and so did Carmen. Several years ago, I had given up the pursuit of "stuff," but for a long time I still clung to the security those things represented. And so did Carmen.

At the start of this adventure, it was easy for me to go out on a limb when I had a safety net under me. But God wanted more. He was asking me to walk a tightrope across Niagara Falls without a pole. Naked. In broad daylight. That's what it felt like.

There have been incredible highs and incredible lows on the road Carmen and I walked—sometimes separately, sometimes side by side—but we wouldn't be the people we are today if we hadn't walked it. Some days I have to laugh when I think of all the time I spent trying to get her to change and all the time she spent trying to get me to change. Meanwhile, God was working to change both of us. What happens next? Only God knows, and only time will tell.

Epilogue

To the Scholarship Committee:

The reason I am so dedicated to television production and communication studies is my dad. An executive in television for more than 15 years, he facilitated the syndication of shows such as Seinfeld, Married With Children, *and* Party of Five. *Ultimately, though, he left the corporate world behind to find something more—and what he found is the reason he is my hero. For the past three years, he has been working to take a little-known story of hope and faith and tell it to as many people as possible. In 2006, three Mexican fishermen were rescued near the coast of Australia after being lost at sea in the Pacific Ocean for more than nine months. When one of them was asked how they survived, he didn't respond with a tale of elaborate planning and fishing techniques— he simply pointed to his Bible. My dad now has the rights to their story and has been working tirelessly to turn it into a book and a movie. His faith and dedication to this story inspires me every single day, but this work*

*has taken a financial toll on our family. He has not had
a salary in several years, yet he encouraged me to apply
to this great university, knowing in his heart that it was
the school of his daughter's dreams. I would not be here
today if it were not for him.*

My oldest daughter gave me the greatest gift a dad
could receive. In an essay for a college scholarship, she
had written from her heart. She had been watching. All
of it. She saw something I lose track of sometimes. She
saw my faith. She saw her mom's faith. She saw the faith
of the fishermen. She saw the faithfulness of God. She
saw the healing. It was being lived out in front of her, and
she was seeing it. It was something *greater* than I could
have imagined and not all that much *later* than I ever
could have hoped for.

I had never written a book before, so, naturally, I
have never written an epilogue. I looked up the word on
Wikipedia—who uses a dictionary these days? (that's so
1990s)—and it said: "An epilogue is a final chapter at the
end of a story that often serves to reveal the fates of the
characters."

I don't know what the fate of anything is, but I am still
alive and working to tell this story in every form I can—
writing, film, speaking—to as many people as will listen. I
love to share this story with a live audience because I get
to look into the eyes of the people listening. I see the pain
in the eyes of the men, a pain that can be healed whether
or not the cause of that pain has long since passed out of
this world or lives two towns over. I get to see the hope
in the eyes of the women who have remained strong for
so long that they have forgotten what it's like to breathe

a sigh of relief from it all. Our marriage is by no means perfect, but Carmen and I are in the best place we have been in twenty years, and while we owe lots more money than we have and I have spoken to the IRS way more than anyone should, we still have a roof over our heads. Our girls are healthy, and the trajectory of their lives has changed in tremendously important ways. My mom is living out her years surrounded by the people she gave so much of herself to: her children and great-grandchildren. I haven't heard from my dad in almost two years, and if we do see each other again, I hope to be able to extend to him a piece of the grace I've been given and simply see him the way God does. The *Tres Pescadores*—Jesús, Salvador, and Lucio—are still fishermen, just like they were before, except now everyone in Mexico recognizes them wherever they go. In the end, I think their legacy will be their faith.

I completed this book a little more than six years from the day God broke the stone around my heart and made me feel like I was living for the first time, three and a half years after I felt the call to go to Mexico, and just a few weeks after God pulled my marriage out of a nose-dive. My daughter's words, part of the harvest, matter more to me than any book or movie ever could. She and her little sister are my legacy. Carmen's legacy. Our legacy.

JK

Acknowledgements

There are so many to thank. First, to my wife Carmen and my daughters, who love me in spite of myself, thank you, thank you, thank you. Joshua, whose prayers started me on this journey with the Creator; and Allison, his wife, who is my friend, co-writer, and the funniest person I know. Howard, who has been there through thick and thin. My friend Victoria, who introduced me to the story of the fishermen and prayed for my safety, knowing that it was probably more dangerous than I ever realized. Her nephew Eli, who helped me not only with translation but also with prayer. The people who helped me in Mexico: Armando, Josefina, Silverio, Eduardo, David, and the staff at Casa Manana. The reporters who asked all the right questions and sometimes gave their own answers.

My in-laws, Don and Millie. My brother-in-law Jeff, who helped me get started. All those who have shared their treasure to help advance this story: Rocky, David, Bert, Fran, Chris, John, Charlie, Van, and Keith. Reed, who is responsible for getting this book finished by kicking me in the behind. Don, Spiros, Graham, and

Rodrigo, who all have worked to get a movie of this story made. Andrew, the best guy I ever hired. My editor, Al, who saved you all from having to read too much (I wouldn't let him edit this part out). Bill, for his keen eye. Everyone in my small groups: Keith, Todd, Charlie, and John. Their wives: Leigh, Celia, Kay, and Susan. Mark and Alice, Van and Susan, Reid and Hope, and Frank and Susie. The group of guys I met through Adventures of the Heart: Reese, Lee, Robert, Chris, Maury, Ron, Brack, Jim, Spencer, Gene, and so many more. Jim, who did us a favor by not stepping in. Our pastor Andy and his father Charles and everyone at Northpoint and In Touch Ministries, who are so gifted at being messengers of the Word. Jeff and Billy and the staff at Buckhead Church for doing all you do to lead people into the most important relationship they will ever have. Paige, Betsy, Beth, Tammy, and Hannah, for watching over my babies as friends and mentors. Gabe and his crew, who are amazing with their connector skills. Paul, for showing me that there really is no business model for this kind of thing. GOD IS THE MODEL. Spiros, for his vision and his friendship, and for his reminders of when the old Joe shows up on the tough days. For all those who let us use their homes to think and write: Keith, Lever, Mark, Ron, and Deborah. Cec, Fox, Bart, Pepper, Shaunti, and Jeff, for the contribution of their words. My friends and colleagues who are part of old Joe—what I like to call B.C.—Terry, Barry, Ed, Susan, Steve, John, and Greg. My mom and dad. You did the best you could. It was hard, I know, and I am thankful that you stayed together for my sake for all those years. My sister and brothers. The tens of thousands of people who prayed for us, loved us, introduced us to someone we needed to meet, supported our efforts in all of this, and chose to be our friends.

Finally, and above all else, Father, Son, and Holy Spirit, who love me, guide me, and dwell in me. They gave me a second life, which I certainly didn't deserve.

Peace,
JK

Author Bio

Joe Kissack is a speaker, author, screenwriter, film and television producer, publisher, and entrepreneur. He has worked on a farm, cleaned out refrigerated swinging beef trucks, and served as a senior executive at Sony Pictures. He often says, "I'm not the king of the world, but I know who is," which is the title of his next book. He is also working on a film about the *Tres Pescadores* called *ALPHAOMEGA*. He lives in Atlanta with his wife of 24 years, Carmen, and their two daughters.

www.thefourthfisherman.com

We want to hear from you.
Please share your thoughts by writing to:

information@thefourthfisherman.com

Have Joe Kissack, author of
The Fourth Fisherman, speak at your event!
For options on booking Joe as your speaker contact:

speakerinfo@thefourthfisherman.com

Speaking Categories Include:

Youth
Arts and Culture
Business/Corporate
Health
Inspirational
Leadership
News Media
Recovery
Men
Charitable Events

For additional information go to:
www.thefourthfisherman.com